It Happened In
South Dakota

It Happened In Series

It Happened In
South Dakota

Remarkable Events That Shaped History

Patrick Straub

Guilford, Connecticut

Project editor: David Legere
Map: M.A. Dubé © Morris Book Publishing, LLC

Library of Congress Cataloging-in-Publication Data is available on file.
ISBN 978-0-7627-5444-1

Printed in the United States of America

10 9 8 7 6 5 4 3 2 1

To all those who call South Dakota home.

CONTENTS

SOUTH DAKOTA

NORTH DAKOTA

NEBRASKA

IOWA

Sioux City

Sioux Falls

Mitchell

Aberdeen

Pierre

Rapid City

Wall

Mount Rushmore

Sisseton/ Lake Traverse Indian Reservation

Flandreau Indian Reservation

Yankton Indian Reservation

Crow Creek Indian Reservation

Lower Brule Indian Reservation

Rosebud Indian Reservation

Pine Ridge Indian Reservation

Standing Rock Indian Reservation

Cheyenne River Indian Reservation

Badlands National Park

James River

Vermillion River

Lewis and Clark Lake

Elkhorn River

Missouri River

White River

Lake Oahe

Grande River

Moreau River

Cheyenne River

Cheyenne River

Bad River

White River

Niobrara River

100 MILES

100 KILOMETERS

50

50

LEGEND

1 Mystery in the Mud: The Crow Creek Massacre—1350

2 The La Verendrye Brothers: Their Short-Lived French Claim—1743

3 First Vote West of the Mississippi—1804

4 La Framboise and Fort Pierre: First Permanent Settlement in South Dakota—1817

5 Arikara and Ashley: The First Fight—1823

6 Todd the Lobbyist: Dakota Territory Is Established—1861

7 Custer's Gold! Gold Discovered in the Black Hills—1874

8 Deadwood: South Dakota's Tall-Tale Factory—1876

9 Blown Away: The First Tornado Ever Photographed—1884

10 January Blizzard: South Dakota's Fatal Snow Day—1888

11 The Last Indian: The Death of Sitting Bull—1890

12 Tragedy at Wounded Knee: Massacre and Conquest of the Sioux—1890

13 Capital Complex: Mitchell and Pierre Fight over Seat of Government—1904

14 Too Corny: The World's Only Corn Palace—1921

15 The Greatest Monument Never Finished: Mount Rushmore—1927

16 Pardon, Madam: Poker Alice Saved from Prison—1928

17 Burning Up the Track: "Smokey" Joe Mendel Wins State Track Meet—1931

18 Thirsty? Wall Drug Serves Settlers—1931

19 Rally 'Em Up: The Sturgis Motorcycle Rally Begins—1938

20 Truly Great Badlands: President Roosevelt Creates Badlands National Monument—1939

21 A Mountain of a Monument: Crazy Horse Memorial—1948

22 Power Play: Oahe Dam Is Completed—1962

23 Shaky Year: The Earthquakes of 1964

24 Black Hills Run Brown: The Rapid City Flood—1972

25 Reinjured: Wounded Knee II—1973

26 Gambling in Deadwood: The Wild West Is Still Alive—1989

27 Dances with Hollywood: South Dakota Hits the Big Screen—1989

28 The Great Flood—1993

29 Plane Crash: Learjet Crash Kills Golfer Payne Stewart—1999

30 Roaring Grizzly: Grizzly Gulch Fire Barely Nips Deadwood—2002

CONTENTS

ACKNOWLEDGMENTS

Thanks to all of the citizens of South Dakota, past and present, and to all of the Native Americans whose stories have been passed down and still need to be heard today.

Thanks to the South Dakota State Historical Society, the tribes of South Dakota, and everyone else who helped in the research of this book.

A huge shout-out to my editor, Allen Morris Jones; without him this book would not have happened. Thanks to my publisher, Erin Turner, and Globe Pequot Press. Thanks to Meredith Davis at Globe Pequot for all of her hard work. And, thanks to Melissa Hayes for her work as well.

Thanks to my two dogs, Madison and Ellie, and my four barn cats, Mr. Kitty, Mrs. Kitty, Smokey Toots, and Daisy Dukes, for providing me with breaks from my writing.

And, most important, thanks to my amazing wife, Brandy Moses, for everything she does.

INTRODUCTION

South Dakota is a state with many contrasts. From the fertile farm-lands of the eastern side of the state to the rugged landscape of the Black Hills, the state covers a geographic area that is quite different from most of the other states in the U.S. From the high plains of the northwest corner to the Missouri River lowlands in the south-east corner, the geography of South Dakota is like a mirror of its history—rich and varied.

During the time of the dinosaurs, South Dakota was probably a tropical paradise for triceratops, massive palm trees, and various other forms of life that are now extinct and absolutely foreign to present-day South Dakota. As the dinosaurs disappeared and global climate changes altered the landscape of South Dakota, so did the presence of human life in the state. Early hunters and gatherers found the plains of South Dakota full of wild game, including elk, bison, bear, moose, deer, and more. It was during this time that many early humans built settlements along the Missouri River. Evidence of these settlements can be found in various locations along the river, as the settlers left behind burial mounds, shards of pottery, and stone tools.

When the bow and arrow came into use on the plains of South Dakota, the hunters found life much easier. But it was the subsistence farming of the gatherers that allowed these early ancestors of the Mandan, Hidatsa, and Arikara to survive on the prairies and river bottoms of South Dakota.

After French explorers François and Louis-Joseph La Verendrye explored the area in 1743, the Sioux made their way into South

Dakota. The history of South Dakota would forever be shaped by the presence of the Sioux and, eventually, white settlers.

For the next two hundred years, conflict would ensue between white settlers and the native tribes of South Dakota, with names like Ashley, the Arikara, Crazy Horse, Custer, Fort Sedgewick, Sitting Bull, American Indian Movement (AIM), Wounded Knee, Sherman, and more . . . the list goes on and on.

The current residents of South Dakota take pride in the fact that their state was shaped by the presence of settlers and native peoples. Today the state is home to nine Indian reservations. From the Lake Traverse reservation in the northeast corner to the Pine Ridge reservation near the Black Hills, Native Americans make up nearly 10 percent of South Dakota's population. Five of the state's counties are located entirely within one of the nine reservations.

The Missouri River dissects the state nearly in half from north to south. The Missouri's presence allowed for steamboats to bring goods to the state in its formative years. Today, the river serves to delineate the climate of the state: The land is considerably more arid on the western side of the river than it is on the eastern side. West of the river, ranching and dry-land farming are the main sources of agriculture. East of the river, corn, soybean, and the occasional dairy farm are more common than large-scale ranching.

For travelers, a visit to the state will most certainly mean a trip along Interstate 90, where visitors will notice the presence of many billboards—especially those advertising Wall Drug, a famous landmark in South Dakota.

The Black Hills are located on the extreme western edge of the state. Perhaps the most often visited region of the state by tourists and South Dakotans on holiday, the Black Hills provide a striking contrast to the high plains surrounding them. The Sioux thought of the Black Hills as sacred. At first they were part of the original Great

Sioux Reservation, but a violation of a treaty by the U.S. government allowed white settlers into the Black Hills. That violation is still a contentious part of life today. Despite the sordid history of the settlement of the Black Hills, the area still features many aspects of South Dakota culture. Home to Mount Rushmore, Crazy Horse Memorial, Sturgis, Deadwood, and many other significant locales, the Black Hills are stunning and unique.

Because of their higher elevation—the highest point is over 7,000 feet—the Black Hills receive more precipitation than other areas of the state and thus feature a wide array of flora and fauna. They are home to mule deer, bighorn sheep, elk, mountain goats, and mountain lions. You can also find plenty of tourist-oriented locales such as Reptile Gardens in Rapid City and the gold mine near Lead, where you can try your hand at panning for gold.

The otherworldly Badlands are perhaps the most obvious metaphor for the contrasts that make up South Dakota. This area sticks out like a sore thumb among the flat plains between the Black Hills and the Missouri River. The Badlands are home to prehistoric fossils and the only true wilderness area in the state.

The largest city in the state is Sioux Falls. Despite their proximity to Iowa and Minnesota, the citizens of Sioux Falls are very proud to be South Dakotans, and hold yearly festivals to celebrate their state's history.

But it is the rural areas of South Dakota that truly capture the spirit of this great state. Laura Ingalls Wilder based several of the books in her Little House on the Prairie series on her life in the small town of De Smet. Other literary figures in the state include Black Elk, whose book, *Black Elk Speaks,* is widely known. Black Elk spent a considerable amount of time recording the history of conflict between whites and Native Americans, and explored the true meaning of the Ghost Dance movement.

More recently, South Dakota has been experiencing a shift in its population. Many of the small rural areas are seeing their towns shrink in size as lack of jobs and the climate are forcing people to move into Rapid City, Pierre, and Sioux Falls. Despite this shift, as history has shown, South Dakotans are able to adapt as they continue to preserve life on the plains.

As they have been doing for the past few hundred years, South Dakotans will ensure that there will always be plenty of reason to say with pride, "It happened in South Dakota."

MYSTERY IN THE MUD: THE CROW CREEK MASSACRE

1350

The sun crept behind the bare bluffs of the western horizon. Dozens of earth lodges sat atop a high bank on the shores of the Missouri River, overlooking the river. The lodges made up Crow Creek village. Men worked in the fields of maize, beans, and squash, tending their crops with tools made from the shoulder of a buffalo or the antlers of a deer. While the men were in the fields, women and children tended to the earth lodges, each one made of posts and beams cemented together with a mud-and-grass mixture. They looked like brown domes with holes cut in the top, and on this late autumn day, soft plumes of smoke escaped from each lodge.

Outside of Crow Creek, the villagers had created a large ditch that served as a fortification for their village. On one side of the village the Crow Creek flowed, nearly fifty feet straight down a steep bank of cliffs. On the other side, the ditch and Wolf Creek created a barrier against any unwanted visitors or raiders. The villagers also dug horseshoe-shaped depressions called bastions from which they could defend their villages.

But on this late fall day with a crisp chill in the air, Crow Creek erupted in violence. The fortification ditch had never been fully completed, allowing the raiders to easily pass through. Armed with bone knives, crude bows and arrows, and blood on their minds, the attackers showed no mercy. Once through the bastions, the attackers had an easy time overtaking the villagers of Crow Creek.

The raiders set fire to the earth lodges, which burned like tinderboxes after years of drought. They pillaged what little food was left in Crow Creek. They tortured and mutilated their victims by scalping, decapitation, cutting off tongues, breaking teeth and jawbones, and other forms of dismemberment. Many villagers were shot with arrows, and some were even burned. Many fled in terror, only to be caught and tortured. Nearly 500 villagers died during the massacre or as a result of the violence.

The attackers took body parts as trophies, and what was not taken as booty was dragged away by coyotes, wolves, and other scavengers. The carnage was widespread and indiscriminate—women and children were not spared. Most of the bodies were placed in the fortification ditch, piled as deep as four feet. While in this mass grave, the bodies remained available as a food source for scavengers. The villagers of Crow Creek suffered a gruesome and uncelebrated death at the hands of vicious attackers, whose identity and motivation remains a mystery to this day.

What is not a mystery is the origin of the Crow Creek village. These villagers had not always lived in Crow Creek. They moved from areas further south, in what are now the states of Iowa, Kansas, and Nebraska, while the earlier residents of Crow Creek moved north to what is now North Dakota and Minnesota. The fertile lands along the two creeks created ideal farming conditions, and the amount of game provided fine hunting. The Crow Creek settlement grew quickly, and soon was home to nearly 8,000 residents. Occasional battles would occur with other villages or nomadic raiders, and every few years the previous residents of Crow Creek would raid the village. The raids and battles became more frequent as regional food supplies dwindled and the area's population continued to boom. The land and game supply could not sustain this population explosion, and several years of drought brought even greater pain to the Crow Creek villagers.

The magnitude of bloodshed at Crow Creek lay locked in the earth until 1978, when archaeologists toured the area. Engineers were excavating a site for a dam on the Missouri River when they discovered human bones. Centered in one location, the large-scale grave had been mostly untouched since the massacre.

Archaeologists have studied the skeletal remains from the mass grave, which reveal evidence of widespread malnutrition. The most obvious sign was pitting on the skulls, above the eye sockets and on the back of the head. The Crow Creek villagers were much shorter than their neighbors, especially the females. Excavators also found the remains of animals with the human remains—all with signs of malnutrition and illness.

As if the ongoing malnutrition was not bad enough, the skeletal remains also show signs of multiple battles and violent warfare. Many of the victims in the mass grave appear to have suffered previous scalpings or arrow punctures that had been healing.

The cause of the massacre and the identity of the attackers remain open to discussion. Several theories hold merit. One suggests that an outside group from the east or west, perhaps traveling Middle Missouri villagers, came through the area and attacked. This theory is not the strongest because of the size of Crow Creek's village. Evidence also suggests that their fortification ditch was not complete at the time of the massacre, which left them open to attack. Relatives of Crow Creek residents lived in nearby villages, which suggests that surely the Crow Creek villagers would have been forewarned about the attack. (In fact, some evidence does imply that the people of Crow Creek did indeed know about their impending doom, but were unable to complete their bastions and defend against attack—perhaps because they were too weak from malnutrition.)

Another theory—the most accepted among experts—is that overpopulation and prolonged droughts and cold winters caused competition from nearby villagers, who envied Crow Creek's location. Several neighboring villages could have combined forces to overtake Crow Creek, as their residents were also experiencing similar malnutrition problems.

The Crow Creek massacre is a well-studied event and archaeological site that provides valuable information about early life on the American plains. Clues to overpopulation, warfare, torture, and interaction between villagers were all exposed because of the massacre.

The remains of the Crow Creek victims have been studied at length. At the request of members of the Crow Creek Sioux tribe, the bones of the victims have been reburied. Members of the tribe oversaw much of the excavation and played prominent roles in the reburial. The victims of the mass grave have been laid to rest, along with the mystery of who caused such massive bloodshed on that cool fall day over 500 years ago . . . and why.

THE LA VERENDRYE BROTHERS: THEIR SHORT-LIVED FRENCH CLAIM

1743

François La Verendrye laced up his cowhide boots, covered his face in a fox-fur scarf, put his head down, and fought the heavy snow with each step. His brother, Louis-Joseph, followed close behind, placing his feet in the large depressions François's boots made in the snow. Louis-Joseph's arms were full of steel beaver traps, and François was dragging the snare lines along behind him in the snow, leaving a single-line impression in the white powdery coldness.

Having left their fur trading post near Lake Superior, the two French explorers were now facing an early spring blizzard. The two men tied a rope between them because the blowing snow was so thick and white they couldn't see ten feet in either direction, which made travel slow. What little food they had brought with them was frozen against their bodies. Eventually the blizzard stopped and François and Louis-Joseph regained their strength and enthusiasm. Their mission: to find the Northwest Passage and harvest animal pelts along the way.

As Americans along the East Coast became wealthier and more sophisticated, the desire for beaver pelts grew. Most pelts were made into beaver hats, worn by elite businessmen. As wealth spread in America, the beaver trade extended further west. The promise of significant returns for prime beaver pelts led to the need for a new water route across North America—the Northwest Passage.

The La Verendrye brothers—the first Europeans to visit South Dakota—rode ambition and hardiness from their homes in France to the Great Lakes. During their journey west from Lake Superior they met Arikara and Mandan peoples in present-day South Dakota along the Missouri River. Interactions with these Indian tribes were peaceful, and ultimately productive, as the brothers learned of new beaver grounds. The brothers were also told of a large mountain range, not to be visited in winter, lying to the west of the flatter lands along the Missouri River.

Their ambition to find the Northwest Passage led the explorers further west, and they trapped beaver, fox, otter, and muskrat along the way. When they reached the Black Hills, the brothers decided to turn back because of the bounty they had previously seen. They knew of plenty of trapping areas along their route and had seen enough beaver to provide wealth for years to come.

By now winter was releasing its grip. The brothers noted the vastness of the plains and the abundance of wild animals. They were impressed, and on their return route, on a hill near present-day Pierre, the explorers deemed the land worthy of French claim. They were granted the authority to claim the lands for France, and on March 30, 1743, one of the brothers etched the following into a one-eighth-inch-thick lead tablet: PLACED BY THE CHEVALIER DE LA VER-ENDRYE, WITNESSES LOUIS-JOSEPH, LA LONDETTE AND A. MINOTTE, THE 30TH OF MARCH 1743.

They then covered the buried tablet with a pyramid of stones, which sat untouched for many years after the brothers left the Missouri River, and perhaps never would have been discovered if not for a group of bored teenagers out for a Sunday-afternoon stroll.

In February of 1913, several teenagers decided they wanted a better view of Fort Pierre. As they walked up a bluff overlooking the river and the town below, Harriet Foster stumbled over an object sticking out of the ground. Along with Foster, George O'Reilly, Leslie Stroup, and the rest of the teenagers scraped off over a hundred and fifty years' worth of dirt. Because the tablet was in French, the kids couldn't read what it said, so they assumed it was junk. The boys immediately decided to sell it for scrap. Fortunately, someone who knew French intercepted them, and ultimately determined the value of the tablet.

French is rarely spoken in South Dakota today, but it may have been if not for the Louisiana Purchase and President Thomas Jefferson. In the years that followed the Purchase, many French-Canadians ventured into South Dakota. The most notable was Pierre Dorion. He settled along the Missouri River near present-day Yankton and married a Nakota woman. Dorion was perhaps the area's first permanent white settler. The French-Canadians who settled in the area traded with the Ponca, Dakota, and Arikara tribes. British traders eventually traveled the Missouri River, making it as far north as the Mandan villages, in what is now North Dakota, creating a land route to the fertile trapping grounds of the Great Plains.

Today, the tablet left by the La Verendrye brothers rests in the Museum of the State Historical Society in the Cultural Heritage Center in Pierre—a site not far from the original bluff, where the brothers chose to mark the property of France. Time and history proved the bluff would ultimately become the property of the United States, and, more specifically, the property of the citizens of South Dakota.

FIRST VOTE WEST OF
THE MISSISSIPPI

1804

The day began like many others for the members of the Corps of Discovery—rising before dawn, readying the keelboat, and preparing for another grueling upstream battle with the river's swirling currents. Captains Meriwether Lewis and William Clark had been discussing their visit with the Oto and Missouri Indians at Council Bluff, near present-day Omaha, Nebraska. This visit was the first official meeting between people from the United States and members of a western Indian tribe. But, it wasn't this meeting that caused concern for the leaders of the Corps.

A few days earlier, Sergeant Charles Floyd had written in his journal, "I am very sick and have been for some time, but have recovered my health again." Despite his optimistic nature, things turned south again shortly, as Floyd became even more ill, unable to write in his own journal. On August 20, Sergeant Floyd died—with a great deal of composure, according to Clark.

Clark diagnosed the cause of death as severe abdominal pain. Modern doctors and historians have surmised that Floyd probably died of a ruptured appendix that had been plaguing him for weeks. The brief upturn he described in his journal was most likely due to the bursting of the appendix, but the inflammation in his abdomen proved to be fatal. Doctors and historians agree that even if Floyd had been in a hospital, most physicians at the time would have been powerless to prevent his death.

Losing their quartermaster and chief navigator was a serious problem, and the Lewis and Clark expedition knew they needed to remedy the situation immediately. After an evening funeral and Floyd's burial, the Corps traveled for a few days and eventually found themselves nearly 20 miles upstream of Floyd's burial site, on a bluff overlooking the Missouri River. The morale of the men was low, but this would quickly change.

While breaking camp the Corps was astounded by the number of elk. The bluff was surrounded by large stands of timber and a creek bottom, which was a main pathway for elk. In fact, local tribes often referred to the area as "Elk Point." In August of 1804, Lewis and Clark tied their boats on the riverbank and ventured inland. In addition to herds of elk, the Corps also found buffalo and deer. After a successful hunt, the men returned to camp, ready for a feast.

As the men prepared their game that evening, Lewis and Clark debated over who to choose as Floyd's replacement. As the campfire blazed and the men enjoyed fresh buffalo steaks, the leaders of the Corps decided to leave the decision up to the men of the expedition. The Corps had a wide array of options in William Bratton, Patrick Gass, and George Gibson, their three nominees.

William Bratton was over six feet tall and had apprenticed as a blacksmith. It is likely that he often assisted the Corps' chief blacksmith, John Shields. Like the other members of the expedition, he earned five dollars a month.

Patrick Gass was a carpenter by trade, but had served in the military for nearly five years. He was not overly tall at five foot seven, and was often described as being a tad risqué when it came to his enjoyment of tobacco and liquor. He was also often accused of having language better suited for a campfire or the deck of a sailing ship than a dinner table. When Gass had first enlisted in the Corps, his commanding officer didn't want to release him from service, as he was not only a fine soldier but also a first-rate carpenter. Eventually, the officer changed his mind, and Gass was allowed to enlist.

George Gibson brought a diverse background to the expedition. He was raised in Pennsylvania but had made his home in Kentucky prior to the expedition. He was described as a skilled hunter and woodsman, and his shooting skills had earned him his place in the Corps. The men enjoyed his fiddle playing (he was one of two members who played the fiddle). His sign language skills proved to be very useful along the way as he could act as interpreter when they met Indian tribes, and the men generally enjoyed Gibson's company.

With the nominees announced, the men of the Corps were about to vote for the first official to be elected by U.S. citizens west of the Mississippi—and what a way to do it, with their stomachs full of fresh buffalo steak. When the votes were tallied, Gass had received nineteen votes, enough for a majority.

Gass proved to be a fine replacement for Floyd, having gained the respect of the members of the Corps. Gass served as one of several journal keepers, right from the beginning of the journey. Others who kept journals included Lewis, Clark, Floyd, John Ordway, and Robert Frazer. Nathaniel Pryor and Alexander Willard may have kept journals as well, but no record exists today.

Gass was a somewhat surprising choice to replace Floyd, given that he admitted to having had only nineteen days of formal education. He described himself as having "never learned to read, write, and cipher till he had come of age." What he may have lacked in formal education, he made up for in experience and maturity. Gass was thirty-three when he joined the Corps, making him one of the oldest members of the group. Clark, Shields, and Charbonneau were the only members older than Gass.

Gass's journal is often considered to be one of the most descriptive and well-written of the entire Corps. Because of his background as a carpenter, his observations of the earth lodges and canoes of the native tribes proved to be important in understanding their construction and materials. He even credited the Skillute Indians with making the finest canoes in the world. After the expedition Gass published his journal before either Lewis or Clark. Gass is credited with titling his journals "The Corps of Discovery of the Great Northwest Expedition," which an editor at the *Pittsburgh Gazette* promptly cut to "The Corps of Discovery."

While on the expedition Gass oversaw the construction of all the winter forts. He made early and constant modifications on the keelboat, allowing for ease of travel and for a shallower draft. He worked with the men in the hewing of the dugout canoes at Mandan, White Bear Island, and Canoe Camps. He designed and built the wagons that were used for the 18-mile portage of the Great Falls. He even assisted Lewis in his experiments with the iron boat frame, but was not responsible for its failure. (A lack of sufficient material to create a proper seal on the seams of the hides was the cause.)

On the return route, Lewis and Clark's faith in Gass was proven even more. As Clark took a regiment of men down the Yellowstone and Lewis took three men to explore the northern boundary of the Louisiana Purchase, Gass was responsible for the remainder of the

Corps. He was to travel the Missouri River and join up later with Lewis and Clark, which he did successfully.

After the expedition Gass returned to West Virginia. He fought in several wars and married a young woman when he was sixty years old. Outliving his wife and even Jean Baptiste Charbonneau (Sacagawea's son), Gass was the last member of the Corps to die, at the age of ninety-nine.

During his lifetime, Gass would vote for eighteen presidents and witness many great events. But for South Dakotans, and for democracy in the United States, perhaps one of the most important elections was the one that took place on August 20, 1804, when Gass was chosen to replace Charles Floyd in the Corps of Discovery.

LA FRAMBOISE AND FORT PIERRE: FIRST PERMANENT SETTLEMENT IN SOUTH DAKOTA

1817

The waters of the Missouri River flowed brown with mud, and chunks of debris floated in the wide river like meat in a frothy stew. Storm clouds grew on the western horizon. This windswept region of the Great Plains, cut by the wide Missouri River, was also home to plentiful beaver—a sought-after species for trappers and traders. Beaver pelts commanded a high price back in the East.

Trapper Joseph La Framboise had heard stories of the great trapping in the Missouri River region, so he'd set out from Chicago in hopes of establishing a fur trading post. On this day he fought the heavy currents and ankle-deep mud of the region's largest river as he followed the path of Lewis and Clark.

In this same location thirteen years earlier, the Corps had had an incident at the mouth of what they called the Teton River, now known as the Bad River. Clark had been traveling slightly ahead of the crew, while a council of Teton Sioux had been following the

Corps. Eventually the Sioux intercepted their path at the mouth of the creek. When Clark drew his sword, Teton chief Black Buffalo calmed everyone's tensions and a skirmish was avoided.

La Framboise knew of the incident, and he also knew that it was important to build a post at the juncture of two bodies of water. His family roots were in fur trading and trapping. His mother, Madeline La Framboise, was one of the most successful trappers and traders in the expansion of the American West. She originally ran the business with her husband, but he was murdered when Joseph was only one year old. Madeline had taught her sons and daughters to speak several languages, including French, English, and local native languages. Because of his mother, Joseph thought success would come easy for him in his trapping and trading ventures.

La Framboise had some experience from building trading posts in Minnesota, so he thought establishing a trading post along the Missouri River would be easy. He was the first white fur trapper to venture into the area with visions of establishing a post. But, as he fought the muddy currents and mucky banks, he struggled more and more with the elements. His boots were soaked, his pants were drenched, and his hands were bloody and raw from the caking mud and thorny reeds. The weather had turned worse even as the mud grew deeper. By nightfall, La Framboise's mood had soured. Not wanting to venture any further into the darkness, La Framboise gathered driftwood, fallen logs, and reeds. Throughout the night he built a crude driftwood and mud shelter, keeping the wind and rain from pounding him all night.

In the morning La Framboise awoke to a clear blue sky. He climbed the banks of the river, which allowed him to see the wide horizon. He saw only much of the same—rolling hills, coulees, and the wide Missouri River. Here, at the confluence of the Bad River and the Missouri River, Joseph began to expand on his driftwood shelter. He created a more permanent building for his residence, and also built a trading post. Whether he chose the site specifically, or was forced to stop there because of bad weather and poor morale, La Framboise's driftwood shack and subsequent trading post became the first permanent settlement in South Dakota, eventually becoming Fort Pierre and the present-day town of Fort Pierre (population 1,900).

In less than a year the post became known as Fort Tecumseh. Indian tribes, trappers, and traders used this central post to transport beaver pelts, buffalo hides, and other items along the river. Due to the Missouri River's changing channels and high water, Fort Tecumseh was later destroyed, and Fort Pierre Chouteau was erected. The new post was built by the American Fur Company and quickly became the largest fur trading post on the upper Missouri River. It also became the central fort for European settlement in the region.

Fort Pierre Chouteau was one of the most productive posts of the American Fur Company. Because of its location on the Missouri River, it received frequent visitors. The fort contained many houses, stables, woodsheds, a sawmill, a milk- and icehouse, and plenty of storage space for gunpowder. For defense, the fort had two fortified bastions.

In time, buffalo hide and robes outnumbered the beaver pelts being traded at the fort, with an average of 17,000 buffalo robes traded each year. Most robes were traded for guns or shot, but a single good-quality robe could be traded for a supply of tobacco, blankets, cloth, sugar, salt, coffee, beads, and gunpowder. At times there were hundreds of Indian tepees surrounding the fort, their occupants waiting to trade goods.

The fort operated as a trading post into the mid-1800s. Today, there are few remnants of Fort Pierre Chouteau. In fact, most of the remaining evidence of the original trading post has been excavated in annual South Dakota State Historical Society archaeological digs. What was once Joseph La Framboise's last-ditch effort to build a shelter for himself surpassed his original ambition, becoming not only a fur trading post, but also the first permanent settlement in South Dakota.

ARIKARA AND ASHLEY:
THE FIRST FIGHT

1823

The group of Arikara men came home early from their morning hunt, unsuccessful in their quest for deer, elk, or buffalo. While they rested from their dawn awakening and several miles hiked on foot, the women of the tribe tended their crops of maize, beans, squash, sunflowers, and tobacco. Things in the village were peaceful on this early summer morning. The village sat on a high bank overlooking the Missouri River. This location allowed the villagers to have constant watch over the river, which was becoming an excellent trapping and trading route for the white settlement nearby.

This band of Arikara enjoyed a subsistence living in their village of earth lodges. They spent much of their time trading agricultural goods with other tribes for meat and hides. The Arikara called the plains of South Dakota home for many years before the Sioux arrived from Minnesota. Despite the Sioux's encroachment into the Arikara's homelands, the two tribes were able to get along peacefully, with only a few skirmishes. The two tribes depended on each other: The

Sioux needed the Arikara for produce, and the Arikara needed the Sioux for meat and hides. However, the Sioux would often bully and force the Arikara into poor deals, and the Arikara's location placed them in the center of interactions between the Sioux and the white trappers and traders.

In fact, during the spring of 1823, a group of trappers had come to the rescue of several Sioux warriors when they were being hunted by a group of Arikara. When the white trappers rescued the Sioux, the Arikara grew even more frustrated with the white settlers, who were encroaching on their territory.

Already disdainful of trappers and traders, the Arikara did not take it lightly when they heard there would be a large trapping expedition, to be led by William Ashley and his business partner, Andrew Henry. The two founders of the Rocky Mountain Fur Company set out on an ambitious journey up the Missouri River and eventually into the Yellowstone River valley. Ashley was known for hiring European and white trappers instead of choosing to hire—or even to barter with—the area tribes. Members of this expedition included soon-to-be-famous Jim Bridger, the Sublette brothers, Jed Smith, and Ed Rose. Altogether the expedition contained around seventy men, all of them eager to explore the West.

On this morning in May, the fate of the Arikara and the ambition of Ashley and Henry's party would collide in a bloody battle along the banks of the Missouri River.

As the sun rose above the eastern bluffs on the Missouri River, a group of Arikara warriors readied themselves for a fight. Although Ashley's group of trappers had encountered several other tribes on their journey, they had managed to evade violent conflict up to this point. The two groups eventually met in battle, with clouds of dust billowing in the air for hundreds of feet as several hundred Arikara and the group of trappers clashed along the Missouri River.

The Arikara were armed with bows and arrows, but they also had fuzil muskets from London, which they had learned to fire with accuracy and efficiency. They also defended themselves with axes and stones.

When the dust had settled, twelve members of the expedition lay dead alongside a few Arikara. The small group of traders proved no match for the hundreds of Arikara warriors, and the remaining survivors fled downstream in the cold, fast, and muddy currents of the Missouri River. The Arikara were victorious—if only for a short while.

The remaining members of the expedition set up a small camp further downstream of the battle site. Ashley sent word of the battle to the U.S. Army in St. Louis and asked for military assistance. It didn't take long for army colonel Henry Leavenworth to send 200 soldiers, and to enlist 750 Sioux and nearly 50 trappers to seek revenge against the Arikara. By the time Leavenworth's group of fighters arrived in early August, the number of men surpassed 1,100.

This army attacked a band of Arikara on August 9, killing nearly fifty members of the tribe. Six days later, they burned an Arikara village. As if to spite the Arikara even more, Leavenworth's men built a post on the former site of the village—a sign to the other tribes in the area that the U.S. Army was there to stay. There were many more incidents between the Arikara and the U.S. Army, but no matter what they did, Leavenworth and his massive numbers were unable to reduce the animosity that existed between the Arikara and the encroaching settlers.

Because the Arikara still considered the Missouri River and its surrounding terrain to be their homeland, the river never developed into a major fur trading route; the area was simply too dangerous for trappers and traders because of the Arikara.

Less than two decades after the fight with Ashley, the Arikara faced a devastating battle with smallpox. Reduced to smaller numbers by the disease, as well as a dwindling food source, the Arikara were forced from their lands along the Missouri River by the Sioux. By the 1870s, nearly all the Arikara in South Dakota had migrated north to present-day North Dakota, where they joined with the Hidatsa and Mandan tribes.

Then, a strange twist: Because they needed jobs, and protection, many Arikara men enrolled at Fort Stevenson as scouts, and several even joined General Custer on his Black Hills Exploration, and eventually went with him to Little Bighorn. Three Arikara scouts—Little Brave, Bobtail Bull, and Bloody Knife—were killed in the Battle of Little Bighorn. Today, most remaining Arikara live with Hidatsa and Mandan tribes on the Fort Berthold reservation in North Dakota.

Ashley tried desperately to keep his fur trading business afloat, despite losing some of his best men as they ventured out on their own or joined other expeditions. Henry resigned from the company, leaving Ashley without a field captain. Undaunted, Ashley organized another group of trappers and traders and headed west on horseback. Because of his fight with the Arikara and other reported skirmishes along the Missouri River, Ashley chose a land route west instead of along the river. By doing this, he was able to explore other regions of the West, including the Colorado River Valley, the Great Salt Lake, the Bighorn Mountains, and other prominent western regions.

In 1826 Ashley sold his interest in the fur trading company and became a supplier for other trading companies rather than continuing as a trader himself. This made his life less risky and more profitable. Ashley ran for governor of Missouri, but lost twice. He was, however, elected as a state senator after the incumbent was shot in a duel. He died in 1838 in Missouri and was buried on a bluff overlooking the Missouri River.

TODD THE LOBBYIST: DAKOTA TERRITORY IS ESTABLISHED

1861

The wagon train was loaded with enough supplies for several weeks. The young town of Yankton was in a flurry of excitement as they prepared to send off their founder, John Blair Smith Todd. Yankton's own young and ambitious lawyer loaded into one of the wagons and settled in for a long and dusty ride east. His journey would take him through Minnesota and Nebraska territories, and on his return trip, he would travel through the Dakota Territory.

Todd had served in the U.S. Army for nearly twenty years before returning to Yankton, the town he had founded. He set up a well-respected law office and enjoyed a fulfilling career. But the hardworking retired army officer desired more. As settlers ventured into the areas around Yankton and points further west, Todd and his fellow citizens were looking for answers and assistance to drought, conflicts with Native Americans, and the toils of life on the frontier. Additionally, when Minnesota became a state, most of the lands east of the Missouri River fell into disarray because the U.S. government couldn't administer the massive geographic area.

The Yankton Treaty took much of the land that had been granted to the Lakota tribe and gave it to the U.S. government. The settlers in the areas that became present-day North Dakota, South Dakota, Wyoming, and Montana were left on their own, with a minimal provisional government. Many of them lobbied for territory status but were continually denied. But a certain lawyer from Yankton had an inside angle—he was cousin-in-law to president-elect Abraham Lincoln. So the young lawyer traveled to Washington, D.C., on behalf of the citizens of his hometown.

Lobbying for territory status was not easy, as the country was gripping for the Civil War. Asking the government to create a territory nearly the size of New England was a stretch, but by using a blend of his strong-willed army skills and his negotiating ability as a lawyer, Todd was able to lobby the United States Congress and his cousin-in-law to create the Dakota Territory on March 2, 1861.

The lands of the new Dakota Territory included the area north of Nebraska Territory, west of Minnesota Territory and the present western border of Wyoming, north to the Canadian border, and west along the Continental Divide in Montana. Because of its establishment as a trading post and central location, Yankton was named as the capital of the Dakota Territory.

Todd was elected to serve as a delegate to the 37th and 38th Congress, representing the Dakota Territory. He served from 1861 to 1865, when he lost his bid for reelection and returned to Yankton. Locally he served as speaker of the territorial House of Representatives in 1866 and 1867. Todd passed away in 1872 in Yankton, but his legacy as the catalyst for the Dakota Territory lives on today.

As an organized territory, the Dakota Territory fell under the jurisdiction of the U.S. government. Because there was now a governing force, much of the lawlessness and vigilante lifestyle tapered off. The Dakota Territory was governed by the Constitution, which granted the citizens within the territory the same rights as those enjoyed by citizens in the country's eastern states. Towns like Deadwood saw more law enforcement and an increase in fair trials, and its citizens were allowed better representation in their own government.

During this time the territory saw some growth, although it was not as expansive as what other territories experienced. This was largely because early settlers encountered the hostile Sioux, who were considered a threat to anyone who ventured into the territory. The U.S. government's violation of several treaties fueled the Sioux's discontent about white settlers' encroachment on land that had originally been granted to them.

In time the Sioux were demoralized and defeated, making the area more attractive to white settlers. The arrival of the Northern Pacific and Chicago & Northwestern railroads increased growth substantially. Many of the settlers came in large groups from other western territories, leaving their entire eastern U.S. villages to start new lives on the frontier. Many Northern and Western Europeans also settled in Dakota Territory, including large numbers of Norwegians, Swedes, and Germans.

The geography of the Dakota Territory was well suited for farming because of the fertile soil and abundant streams. As the population grew, wheat farming, mining, and cattle ranching became the main sources of income for settlers, and when the Black Hills gold rush hit the area, many merchants and hoteliers ventured into the territory as well.

The Dakota Territory remained quite large until 1868, when Montana and Wyoming territories were removed. At that point Dakota Territory was reduced to the present-day boundaries of North and South Dakota.

CUSTER'S GOLD! GOLD DISCOVERED IN THE BLACK HILLS

1874

On this early July day in 1874, the waters of French Creek raced downhill through the forests of the Black Hills. The creek flowed for 62 miles before joining the Cheyenne River, tumbling over rocks, boulders, and small cascades. The waters of French Creek were important for the many deer, bear, and other mammals in the area, but its most important asset was soon to be discovered.

The bright sun beat down heavy on the prairie as men saddled their horses and women readied packs and bags. The soldiers of Fort Abraham Lincoln were preparing for a journey. General George Armstrong Custer was their leader, and their mission was to explore the Black Hills and evaluate possible sites for a fort in or near the Black Hills.

This journey was not without conflict, as the Fort Laramie Treaty of 1868 clearly prohibited settlement or travel through portions of the territory that had been granted to the Sioux. However, Secretary of the Interior Columbus Delano felt differently about the

1868 treaty. Delano was responsible for upholding the territorial rights of the Sioux, and he wrote a letter to Custer expressing his feelings about the treaty:

> *I am inclined to think that the occupation of this region of the country is not necessary to the happiness and prosperity of the Indians, and as it is supposed to be rich in minerals and lumber, it is deemed important to have it freed as early as possible from Indian occupancy. I shall, therefore, not oppose any policy which looks first to a careful examination of the subject. . . . If such an examination leads to the conclusion that [this] country is not necessary or useful to Indians, I should then deem it advisable . . . to extinguish the claim of the Indians and open the territory to the occupation of the whites.*

With Delano having laid the groundwork to open up the area, General Alfred H. Terry at the Department for Dakota Territory headquarters ordered Custer to explore the region.

Custer and his 1,000 troops set out as the midsummer sun warmed the dusty ground of Fort Abraham Lincoln. Clad in his usual buckskin outfit, Custer was at the head of the nearly mile-long procession of infantry troops, scouts, guides, and one cook—a black woman named Sarah Campbell. There were six-mule teams pulling 110 covered wagons, Gatling guns and cannons towed behind horses, and nearly three hundred head of cattle to serve as food for the members of the expedition.

Custer and Terry wanted this expedition to be as well documented as Lewis and Clark's had been. Custer's troops included an entire scientific corps, consisting of a geologist and his assistant, a naturalist, a botanist, a medical officer, a topographical engineer, a zoologist, and a civil engineer. Two miners, Horatio Nelson Ross and William T. McKay, also fell under the jurisdiction of the scientific corps. Custer and Terry also insisted on the following: a photographer; newspaper correspondents; a band; hunting dogs; the son of U.S. President Ulysses S. Grant; and Grant's brothers, Tom and Boston.

Although deemed a military expedition by Terry and Delano, Custer felt otherwise. Each morning as they broke camp, the band entertained the troops. They also provided music in the evenings while many of the men enjoyed an evening meal complete with wine and fine cutlery. This was far from a stress-filled journey.

In mid-July the massive party reached the Belle Fourche River, where they first gazed upon the Black Hills, taking note of the flora and fauna, the cliffs, and the clear, free-flowing streams. They had arrived at the peak of midsummer beauty. Although Custer noted that they found little sign of Indian occupation in the Black Hills, Custer himself may have left his mark atop the 6,380-foot-high Inyan Kara Mountain, which lies in the northwest corner of the Black Hills.

The Inyan Kara is a massive granite uplift in the shape of a mesa covered with pine trees. At the summit is an inscription that reads 74 G CUSTER. This is the same inscription that Custer left on many other summits in the West. However, debate abounds as to whether this was actually done by Custer, or whether it was merely a practical joke performed by local high school students. Records from men who were on the journey do not mention a carving. However, that does not rule out the possibility that Custer did make the inscription; some of his future actions would prove that he liked to do things unconventionally.

Nearly a week after they had crossed the Belle Fourche River, the expedition set up camp along the clear waters of French Creek. The location of their camp was near present-day Custer. Many members of the expedition enjoyed another of their nightly dinner parties to the accompaniment of the band, drinking wine by the campfire before settling in for the night.

The next day the military men planned to venture forth with Custer to find a suitable location for a fort. The scientists and naturalists would continue their cataloging and study of the area's bounty, while the two miners, Ross and McKay, would be on their own to discover whatever they could find.

Custer and his military men set out at sunrise on July 22. Sleeping in a little after a night of steak and wine, Ross and McKay eventually left camp. It was not long before Ross noticed something shiny in the clear waters of French Creek. As he got closer and pulled some of the shiny material from the creek, his suspicions were confirmed—it was gold. He and McKay would eventually find gold in several of the creeks during the remainder of the expedition. It didn't take long for General Custer to send off a dispatch about this first exciting discovery:

> *[G]old has been found at several places, and it is the*
> *belief of those who are giving their attention to this sub-*
> *ject that it will be found in paying quantities. I have*
> *on my table forty or fifty small particles of pure gold . . .*
> *most of it obtained today from one panful of earth.*

Custer sent Charley Reynolds 115 miles to Fort Laramie to spread the word. Reynolds made the journey on horseback in less than four nights. Word was then sent to General Terry in St. Paul.

Terry was astounded to hear of the discovery of gold, but also impressed with the descriptions of the region's mountains and flora and fauna, and the abundance of clear, cold water.

In less than ten days, news of gold in the Black Hills had spread throughout the United States. Back at French Creek, Ross and McKay and other members of the expedition had already created the first official mining claim, and the first official mining company, in South Dakota: District No. 1 for the Custer Mining Company.

The expedition remained in the Black Hills for another month and covered nearly 1,200 miles. Custer would not live to see the massive impact of his 1874 expedition, as he was killed two years later at the Battle of Little Bighorn.

Ross's discovery proved to be paramount in the settlement of the Black Hills. It took only a few years before a full-on gold rush hit the area. The onslaught of fortune seekers antagonized the Sioux of the Black Hills region. Not only had the Sioux been promised this area in the Fort Laramie Treaty—which was violated by Delano— but they also considered the Black Hills to be sacred ground.

For the next five years the United States and the Sioux fought in the Great Sioux War.

DEADWOOD: SOUTH DAKOTA'S TALL-TALE FACTORY

1876

Spurs clinked as boots sauntered across the barroom floor. The piano player banged out popular tunes from a corner of the dusty room. It was a typical busy evening at Nuttall & Mann's Saloon No. 10 in the raucous town of Deadwood. When a tall man with curly hair that fell beyond his shoulders walked in, not everyone in the saloon turned around to see who he was. The barkeep knew him. He knew that this man would choose to sit in the corner of the room, keeping watch for any attack from behind. That's because James Butler Hickok, aka Wild Bill Hickok, slept with one eye open and always watched his back.

Hickok was unable to find a corner seat on this early August day. The hot summer weather meant folks had quit mining early and headed for the saloon. In hopes of even greater fortune, dozens of miners, cowboys, and frontiersmen worked the poker tables. There was not an empty seat in the bar and Hickok was nervous. He compromised and sat with his back to one door so he could at least face another open door. This compromise proved fatal when Jack McCall shot Hickok in the back of the head with a .45 caliber revolver. Wild Bill had been tamed, but the seedy underbelly of Deadwood was just beginning.

Deadwood was founded on lands originally granted to the Sioux. However, because of the breach of the Fort Laramie Treaty by the United States, General George Custer was able to explore the Black Hills area. During Custer's 1,000-member expedition, gold was discovered in a small creek about 60 miles south of Deadwood. As word of gold spread throughout the West and made its way east, prospectors, gunslingers, miscreants, and just about everyone else wanted a piece of the action. Details of the gold findings were hazy, but fortune seekers came nonetheless, and carved out tales of their adventures.

The founding of Deadwood is one of those tales. Two stories exist as to who was the first to discover this rambunctious mining settlement.

In the first account, Deadwood was founded by a group of men led by Ed Murphy, who had come from Montana to visit the gulch in the fall of 1875. They shared reports of finding gold in the area. A year later Frank Bryant stumbled onto more gold on a deer-hunting trip; he returned shortly thereafter with a party of men and began prospecting the gulch. On November 17, 1876, Bryant wrote the following on a spruce tree: "We, the undersigned, claim three hundred feet below this notice for discovery, and nine hundred feet or three claims above this notice for mining purposes." The note was signed "Frank S. Bryant, William Cudney, W. H. Coder."

The second account was first reported in the *Deadwood News* in October of 1880. Dan Meckles and seven other men were sluicing the waters of Castle Creek, and they'd had a run of bad luck. The two quickly dismantled the crate of a wagon they'd been using to haul supplies. After dismantling they took the scrap and built a sluice box. They were disappointed to find less than $10 in gold and were ready to move out of the area. But then Meckles came into camp, boasting of a gulch where gold was found, 50 cents to the pan. At first the men did not believe Meckles and had to see it with their own eyes. The group climbed up and over Bald Mountain and into Deadwood Gulch, so named because of the abundance of dead trees.

Once they were in the bottom of the gulch, Bill Gay panned 50 cents' worth of gold—in essence, the tip of the iceberg from the creek. Soon the others followed suit, all panning with equal success. In the coming months the group built the first cabin in the gulch. Elk and deer were an abundant source of food, the area was full of timber for building and firewood, and there were plenty of creeks to pan for gold—why leave? In fact, they staked their claims and worked each day to find their fortune in the gulches of Deadwood.

In April of 1876 the town of Deadwood was laid by Craven Lee, Isaac Brown, J. J. Williams, and a few others. E. B. Farnum was elected mayor of the young town. Soon after Farnum's election, enterprising frontiersmen and brothers Charlie and Steve Utter arrived in Deadwood with a wagon train full of prospectors, gamblers, prostitutes, and other hopefuls. One of Charlie's more lucrative operations was a delivery service to Cheyenne, Wyoming. His load would regularly contain several hundred to a couple of thousand letters per trip—a testament to the growing interest in Deadwood.

Part of the Utter brothers' wagon train included prostitutes. As a man always looking to fill a void, Charlie Utter realized there was a high demand for women in Deadwood. Many of the prostitutes who traveled with Utter went to work in Deadwood's many brothels. The most well-known and respected madam was Dora DuFran, who owned several brothels during her time in Deadwood, including her most popular, Diddlin Dora's. DuFran was known for requiring her girls to dress well and practice good hygiene. Occasionally, when she was in town, Calamity Jane would be in DuFran's employ.

But DuFran was not without competition in Deadwood. Her toughest competitor was madam Mollie Johnson, known as the "Queen of the Blondes." Johnson had three other blonde girls as protégés, and the four women were often caught up in fighting each other over profits and men. There is little indication that madams DuFran and Johnson disliked each other.

Tom Miller opened the upscale Bella Union Saloon and Theater in the fall of 1876. Town meetings would often be held at the Bella Union, as it was considered one of Deadwood's more reputable establishments.

The use of opium was also a popular pastime in the early days of Deadwood. The Gem Variety Theater, opened in April of 1877 by Al Swearengen, was the hub of the town's opium trade. Swearengen was one of the first residents of Deadwood to dabble in something other than prospecting or mining. His theater would host fights between local miners for citizens to watch and gamble upon, but it was prostitution and his brutal way of doing business that brought him fame. His Gem Variety Theater quickly became the most profitable brothel in town, bringing in as much as $10,000 a night, nearly $180,000 in today's dollars. He and his henchmen would often abuse and bully the prostitutes.

When the Gem Variety burned in September of 1879, Swearengen rebuilt an even larger version. He was adept at creating political alliances, keeping himself above the law for much of his time in Deadwood. His death was less glamorous than his life: He was beaten to death in 1904 by an assailant with a blunt object in a Denver street.

Aside from brothels, drugs, and quick fortune and fame, the town also witnessed the death of Wild Bill Hickok, was home to

Calamity Jane for several years, and saw sheriff Seth Bullock curtail a rowdy citizenry. Bullock quickly deputized several residents to help him rid the town of a majority of the riffraff, without killing anyone. Bullock even went so far as to tell Wyatt Earp that Earp's services were not needed in Deadwood.

Bullock was also an enterprising businessman with partner Solomon "Sol" Star. Bullock and Star had established a relationship during their time together in Helena, Montana. The promise of prosperity had brought them to Deadwood. When their original hardware store burned down in 1894, they decided to rebuild—but instead of another hardware store, they built Deadwood's first luxury hotel, complete with steam heat and indoor plumbing. The Bullock Hotel still operates today. Sol Star was elected to Deadwood's first town council, served as postmaster in 1877, and was elected mayor in 1884, serving in that capacity for fourteen years.

In time Deadwood's rough-and-tumble existence slowed as the gold rush faded and mining became more consistent. A devastating fire in 1879 destroyed over 300 buildings and burned most of the town's residential structures. Without homes and without the promise of gold, many left Deadwood. But four of the town's most prominent citizens still remain, buried in Mount Moriah Cemetery: Wild Bill Hickok, Calamity Jane, Seth Bullock, and Sol Star. All of them keep watch over Deadwood today, making sure its rambunctious roots remain.

BLOWN AWAY: THE FIRST
TORNADO EVER PHOTOGRAPHED

1884

The morning of August 28, 1884, began like many others for the small-town reporter in Aberdeen. He enjoyed his steaming cup of coffee, reread yesterday's dailies, and met with his publisher. Life was normal at the *Aberdeen Saturday Pioneer*. But in Bridgewater, a tiny town south of Aberdeen, trouble loomed in the skies.

This reporter had moved to South Dakota Territory to open "Baum's Bazaar." For a few years business was good, but he soon went bankrupt. His generosity and willingness to extend too much credit to the many homesteaders and pioneers of early South Dakota Territory proved to be his undoing, so shopkeeper-turned-reporter Lyman Frank Baum left the retail business and ventured into writing for the local newspaper. Baum's fate would change forever after the events of August 28 inspired him to write *The Wonderful Wizard of Oz*.

In Bridgewater the day began with clear blue skies and warm sunshine. Farmers tended their corn and wheat crops. Children got ready for school, and homemakers made beds, cleaned house, and did their chores. The temperature seemed unseasonably warm for late August, but people paid little attention to the weather as they went about their business.

As the day wore on and the farmers came close to finishing their work, the sky to the west became heavy with large white clouds. Many of the clouds rose high into the atmosphere, creating a huge, billowy mass that seemed to stretch for miles across and thousands of feet high. In time the western horizon was covered with these large clouds. By early evening the entire sky was a black cauldron of clouds and rain. Even though sunset was a few hours off, the darkness caused by the ominous clouds and oncoming weather made it feel like it was already nighttime. But it wasn't the clouds and the rain that caused people to head for cover; it was the wind, thunder, and lightning that provided a warning sign of the carnage to come. Trees began to bend, and some broke with the sheer force of the wind. Farmers who were not yet inside had to yell to each other in order to be heard, even when standing side by side. Children's screams were muffled by the roar of the wind. Barns and farmhouses began to lose roof shingles in the howling gusts.

Eventually the clouds began to form into a tornado. As the funnel lowered to the ground near Bridgewater, the level of terror increased. With wind gusts of over 50 miles per hour, people ran to hide in ditches or creek beds, or just collapsed into nearby fields to keep from being blown away.

The twister left a path of destruction in its wake, including hundreds of downed trees, several dead livestock, piles of lumber that used to be buildings, and incalculable damage to crops. The tornado was responsible for the deaths of four people, and numerous others were injured in the twister's wrath.

As the tornado moved away from Bridgewater, it traveled slightly north toward Howard, South Dakota. Word of the storm had spread, so there were no further deaths; however, what happened next would have a long-lasting impact.

As the tornado moved across a cornfield, it destroyed everything in its path. Despite the ferocity of the storm, with dust, dirt, and debris circling thirty feet up in the air, one brave soul took the time—and the risk—to capture the tornado in a photograph. This image of the twister descending from the blackened sky, with two smaller twisters forming around the massive funnel as it touched the ground, became the first known photograph of a tornado. Mystery surrounds the identity of the photographer, but the image itself inspired one of the greatest stories of all time.

Further north in Aberdeen, Baum was struggling to find material for his column, "Our Landlady," when news of the tornado started to buzz around the newsroom. Baum knew that he had to see the photograph for himself. Eventually he did, and the deathly image of the black clouds and the treacherous funnel protruding from the sky gave him the inspiration for the tornado that sent Dorothy to Oz.

Since the tragic tornado of 1884, South Dakota has experienced many similar horrific storms. One of the most notable was the Bijou Hills storm that took place fifteen years after the photograph captured the tornado near Howard. This cyclone touched down on Charles Peterson's farm near Bijou Hills on May 29, 1899, killing Peterson and six of his children. His wife and two other children suffered life-threatening injuries. The scene at their farm was gruesome, as body parts were strewn across the farmhouse compound along with tree limbs and farm machinery.

The tornado destroyed several other farmhouses, a church, a schoolhouse, and many other buildings before it dissolved after crossing the Missouri River.

On June 23, 1914, another tornado ripped through Brown County. It destroyed nearly every building on four farms. One man was killed as he helped his family to safety in their cellar; while they survived, he did not. A sister storm that night brought carnage to Watertown, destroying three farms and causing more than $200,000 worth of damage in 1914 dollars.

A little over a hundred years later, death and destruction came to the state again in the form of a tornado. On May 30, 1998, huge clouds formed near Farmer and the winds increased; the storm eventually developed into a twister. As the tornado traveled from Farmer toward Spencer, it destroyed farmhouses, small buildings, and crops. Winds topped 200 miles an hour as the storm roared through Spencer. The tornado left a trail of debris for miles, destroying homes, an apartment complex where six people died as a result of the tornado, and thousands of downed trees and power poles. The storm also spawned several other twisters, but none were as devastating as the tornado that went through downtown Spencer.

The most recent notable tornado happenings in South Dakota were also the most record-breaking. Although not as fatal as previous tornadoes, in the past ten years South Dakota has seen several outbreaks. On June 24, 2003, over 65 tornadoes touched down. Nearly 350 tornado warnings were broadcast, and one observer witnessed 14 tornadoes in that one day. The highest wind speed recorded that day topped 260 miles per hour.

Another outbreak occurred on September 16, 2003, when seven twisters hit ground between 4:00 p.m. and 7:00 p.m. The strongest ran for nearly twenty minutes through McCook County. Although damage was widespread, there were no fatalities.

The most recent outbreak of tornadoes occurred on May 5, 2007. Twenty-five twisters hit ground between 4:00 p.m. and 10:00 p.m. When plotted on a map, the tornadoes were nearly all in a swath from Carthage south through Mitchell and on down to Yankton. Again, there was extensive damage but no fatalities. Near

Yankton a camper-trailer was thrown into a stand of trees. Near Plankinton, an empty car trailer was blown end over end for more than a hundred yards.

In the past hundred years or so, South Dakota has experienced nearly 2,000 twisters. Since 1950, when detailed records were initiated, there have been over 1,500 tornadoes, 20 deaths, and millions of dollars' worth of damage. However, the first tornado ever photographed—the one that inspired events in *The Wonderful Wizard of Oz*—may be the most notable of all.

JANUARY BLIZZARD:
SOUTH DAKOTA'S FATAL SNOW DAY

1888

The morning of Thursday, January 11, 1888, was a quiet one in South Dakota. Children readied themselves for school, relaxed and in no rush. Ranchers enjoyed working outside in the mild winter weather, reveling in the bright blue skies and temperatures in the 60s. Weather like this in January provided a respite from the normal snow and winds of midwinter. On Thursday afternoon children rushed to enjoy snowball fights before all the snow melted. The few remaining snowmen slowly wilted under the bright midwinter sun.

After the mild weather on Thursday, twelve-year-old Lena Tetzlaff was enjoying another day of abnormal winter weather on Friday, January 12. Temperatures were still in the high 30s, and the skies were still a beautiful clear blue. Lena spent the morning of January 12 at her parents' farm in northeastern South Dakota.

Outside Great Plains, South Dakota, two men wearing unseasonably light clothing saddled their horses, ready for another day of nice weather while tending their herd of cattle. The men rode past farmers heading to their fields, merchants walking to work or to market, and schoolchildren on their way to school. The skies to the west were clear and sunny. The breeze was calm. The men felt lucky to be alive on such a beautiful day.

Unbeknownst to the people of South Dakota, there was bad weather in southern Alberta. It had moved into central Montana, and was now preparing to blast South Dakota. In Montana temperatures had plummeted to minus-50 degrees Fahrenheit, and the storm had dumped several inches of snow and already claimed many lives. But the citizens of South Dakota still enjoyed a quiet morning, until midday.

By noon those peaceful blue skies had turned black and deadly. First, there was the driving wind, blowing with fury out of the northwest, whirling dust and snow high into the air and bending trees over double with its force. Livestock lay down in the fields, and farmers and ranchers struggled to see in the swirls of dust, snow, and falling limbs.

Then the snow began to fall in earnest, piling onto tree limbs and causing them to crack and break. It fell with such a fury that many witnesses reported not being able to see their hands in front of their faces. The wind blew the snow into drifts, many higher than the rooftops. Doors were blocked by the immense drifts, and people were trapped inside as well as outside. Any snow that was shoveled was almost immediately replaced with new drifts.

As if the snow and wind were not enough, the temperatures quickly turned fatal. After a day of mild weather on Thursday, people were not prepared for the icy winds and bone-chilling cold. A weather observer in Huron, South Dakota, recorded a northwest wind of 44 miles per hour, with the temperature at minus-2 degrees Fahrenheit and a wind chill of minus-33 degrees. Lena Tetzlaff claimed that the temperature dropped to minus-40, nearly a 60-degree change. Farmers ran from their fields for the shelter of their homes. Some made it, some didn't. Ranchers on horseback galloped in terror through the blinding whiteness to the safety of any available structure. One of the unlucky ranchers was Tetzlaff's cousin, George Tetzlaff, who froze to death while riding his horse back to town.

In Great Plains, the two men who were riding to work were fortunately close enough to town to turn back in time. But on their way back they noticed a schoolhouse full of children. With frozen fingers they tied off their horses. Only able to see five feet in front of them, they found more rope and tied a rope between them. As the snow piled at their feet and the children in the schoolhouse grew more and more terrified in the rapidly dropping temperatures, the men searched for more rope. They finally found several lengths and tied them together to create a long line. With one end of the rope tied to the schoolhouse and the other tied to the nearest house, the men accompanied the children to the safety and warmth of the house—all the while telling the children to not let go. The children were forced to grip the rope tightly and walk slowly, hand over hand, following the rope to safety. As the last child struggled through the wind and drifting snow, the two men stoked the fire. When everyone had made it safely inside, the men closed the door against the storm, and they all settled in for a long night.

By the morning of January 13, the skies had cleared and the wind had calmed. The bitter cold remained for several more days. Many snowdrifts were estimated to be more than ten feet deep. It took days, even weeks, for many people to dig out of their homes. The drifts were so thick and numerous that schoolchildren had to be escorted back to their homes by adults.

Farmers surveyed their fields to inspect the damage. Ranchers searched their land only to find perished livestock. Merchants prayed that their stores had suffered little damage from the wind and cold. It would be weeks before life would return to normal.

The blizzard was caused when an immense mass of arctic air collided with a warm, wet air mass from the Gulf of Mexico. The few days of balmy weather that had preceded the storm indirectly caused many of the deaths. Because of the warm weather, people had traveled farther than normal from their homes, or they were just enjoying the chance to be outdoors in the middle of winter. The blizzard occurred so quickly over the Great Plains that many people were unprepared; there was little they could do to protect themselves, and they paid the ultimate price.

From Montana to Texas, it is estimated that nearly 235 people died as a result of the blizzard. In South Dakota alone, there were an estimated 35 deaths, many of them schoolchildren. When the storm hit the Great Plains on the afternoon of January 12, many schoolchildren were caught outdoors.

In Runningwater, Dakota, Mrs. Wilson left her schoolhouse with nine children, but they never made it to the safety of a nearby house. A day later, all of them, along with Mrs. Wilson, were found frozen to death not far from the schoolhouse.

Mary Matilda Sisson of Douglas County, South Dakota, said that when the snow finally melted, searchers discovered dead horses and cattle across the prairie near their homestead. Once the snowdrifts had thawed, they uncovered bodies of men and schoolchildren.

In Pawnee City, Nebraska, teacher Seymour Dopp kept his seventeen students overnight. They burned wood in the schoolhouse stove to stay warm. The next day parents shoveled through snowdrifts to get into the schoolhouse and rescue their children.

Minnie Freeman, a teacher in Nebraska, led her students to safety after the wind ripped the roof off of her one-room schoolhouse.

Less fortunate than Freeman's students, Lois Royce tried to lead three children to safety in her house. But during the 300-foot journey from the schoolhouse to Royce's home, they became lost in the blinding snow. The three children died and Royce lost her feet to frostbite.

William Saxton of Albion, Nebraska, was filling his sled with hay on the day of the blizzard. As the snow fell and the wind blew, Saxton used a pitchfork to carve out a cave inside the haystack for shelter. The next day, he sent his dog out for help. The dog returned home and led a group of searchers back to Saxton, still shivering in his cave. Saxton's fingers were severely frozen and part of his leg had to be amputated.

In Iowa, Jurgen Jepsen and his family were stranded in one of his cornfields. He had lost his team of horses and only the wagon was left. He overturned the wagon to protect his family and left to find his horses. Mrs. Jepsen grew impatient when Jurgen did not return, and she left to find him. The next day they found her, frozen in the snow less than 100 feet from the overturned wagon. Jurgen was later found with severe frostbite.

The scope of the blizzard is best described by Douglas County, South Dakota, resident Sadie Shaw. A few days after the blizzard, in the comfort of her own home, she wrote the following letter to her eastern relatives: "I have seen the Dread of Dakota—a genuine blizzard—and am now ready to leave anytime, that we can sell. *Oh, it was terrible.* I have often read about Blizzards but they have to be *seen* to be fully *realized.*"

THE LAST INDIAN:
THE DEATH OF SITTING BULL

1890

It began when the great Hunkpapa and Lakota leader Sitting Bull awoke in a cold sweat one night after experiencing his own death in a dream. A proud and visionary leader, Sitting Bull feared for his life after awaking; in the nightmare, his life was ended in an altercation with his own people. His terror proved to be prophetic.

Sitting Bull had been touring with Buffalo Bill's Wild West Show for four months before choosing to return to the Standing Rock Reservation. Once at Standing Rock, Sitting Bull reunited with most of his original band of Lakota and Hunkpapa. During this time Sitting Bull and other Lakota were beginning to practice the Ghost Dance religion, which had been founded on peaceful principles, including the cohabitation of Anglos and Native Americans. However, many homesteaders and members of the U.S. government feared the Lakota were interpreting the Ghost Dance religion to mean a "renewed earth." This meant "washing away all the evil"—and according to the Lakota, the real evil was the intrusion of Anglos on the lands that had once belonged to the Lakota and Hunkpapa peoples.

The U.S. government didn't help matters when it broke a Lakota treaty by changing the boundaries of the Great Sioux Reservation. Breaking this treaty gave the government the power to create five smaller reservations. This separated many families and broke tribal unions. The U.S. policy at the time was to officially disband tribal relationships, peacefully or not, to make room for encroaching homesteaders. Sitting Bull and the Lakota's Ghost Dance religion created unease, justified or not, for the U.S. government.

The Ghost Dance was a dancing ritual performed in a circular fashion that would last until many of the dancers collapsed from exhaustion. Believers felt their physical sacrifice would ensure the return of the dead. Many of the religion's followers had lost husbands, warriors, and friends in battles with the U.S. government. The hope of a renewed relationship with their ancestors sustained their belief in the Ghost Dance.

The religion came from Wovoka, a Paiute Indian "messiah." Sitting Bull and his brother, Short Bull, had visited the mystic. Wovoka's intentions when meeting with Sitting Bull and Short Bull were peaceful, just as the message of his Ghost Dance was all about peace between Indians and Anglos. But as more and more Sioux began to practice the Ghost Dance, homesteaders, Indian Agents, and the U.S. government grew more nervous. Some agents were so afraid of the new dances that they wired Washington, D.C., for more military backup.

One of the Lakota chiefs, Kicking Bear, was a prominent leader in the Ghost Dance movement. Kicking Bear and Sitting Bull were at Standing Rock together. At first, Sitting Bull felt comfortable with the increasing frequency of Ghost Dance rituals, even though he doubted that the dance would actually return the dead to the living. While he had no personal objections to the dances and the religion, the growing anxiety of the homesteaders and soldiers made him nervous as well. Sitting Bull was afraid the U.S. government would be called in to kill more of his band.

Kicking Bear showed less fear. In fact, he encouraged more dancers to wear special shirts with painted "magic" symbols on them; some believed these symbols would repel bullets if the soldiers were to attack.

As fears increased on both sides, so did the amount of Ghost Dances performed and the number of soldiers brought into Standing Rock. Tensions reached a level that approached hysteria as Lakota wore their Ghost Dance regalia nonstop, and soldiers were at the ready around the clock. Eventually Kicking Bear was forced to leave Standing Rock. This had no effect on the number of dancers, or on the amount of dances they performed. The leading agents of the reservation asked for more troops.

Agent Valentine McGillycuddy felt unafraid and seemed to understand the religious ceremonies. A surgeon by trade, McGillycuddy was respected for his insight into the delicate relationship between the Sioux and the U.S. government. After Kicking Bear was removed, McGillycuddy wired his superior officers with his observations:

> *The coming of the troops has frightened the Indians. If the Seventh-Day Adventists prepare the ascension robes for the Second Coming of the Savior, the United States Army is not put in motion to prevent them. Why should not the Indians have the same privilege? If the troops remain, trouble is sure to come.*

As with Sitting Bull's nightmare, McGillycuddy's sentiments would prove to be prophetic.

The majority of the agents felt Sitting Bull was at the root of the dances and responsible for their continued growth. They had blamed Sitting Bull in their formal request for additional troops, and despite the fact that this was a false accusation, their request was granted, and thousands of troops were deployed to Standing Rock.

On December 12 an order was given to arrest Sitting Bull. Two days later an officer from nearby Grand River arrived at agency headquarters with a letter announcing that Sitting Bull was making plans to leave the reservation. The letter stated:

> *That Sitting Bull was making preparations to leave the reservation; that he had fitted his horses for a long and hard ride, and that if he got the start of them, he being well mounted, the police would be unable to overtake him, and he, therefore, wanted permission to make the arrest at once.*

This letter was received and read by Standing Rock agent James McLaughlin. Upon reading this account, McLaughlin felt immediate action was necessary. Two days later, he dispatched a force of thirty-nine Indian policemen and four volunteers, one of which was Sitting Bull's brother-in-law, Gray Eagle.

The posse entered Sitting Bull's camp at daybreak, in a freezing rain. They surrounded Sitting Bull's home, knocked, and entered, telling Sitting Bull that he was under arrest and would be traveling to the agency headquarters. After Sitting Bull had dressed for the journey from his home to agency headquarters, his son Crow Foot began to yell at him. Crow Foot was furious at his father for taking the arrest so peacefully, and demanded that his father stay.

By now, Sitting Bull was fully dressed and ready to go; he had no choice but to walk past his screaming and defiant son. Soon, many members of Sitting Bull's family and tribe were on the scene and curious. In seeing his family and his tribal members in disgust, Sitting Bull grew impatient and refused to mount the horse. The posse tired of Sitting Bull's resistance and used force. As Sitting Bull demanded help from onlookers, the police tried to calm the crowd, and eventually forced them back.

Two different accounts attempt to explain what happened next, but neither provides conclusive evidence. It does seem clear that a large, close-quarters fight resulted. One account says a Sioux, Catch the Bear, shouldered his rifle as the police wrestled with Sitting Bull. Catch the Bear supposedly shot a Lieutenant Bull Head, who then fired his revolver at close range into the chest of Sitting Bull. Upon seeing that, another police officer felt Sitting Bull was not dead enough, so he shot the Sioux chief in the head.

A second account said that Sitting Bull called for the growing crowd of Sioux to attack the police. According to this account, Catch the Bear and Strike the Kettle exploded from the crowd and fired at Lieutenant Bull Head, who, at the time, was standing next to Sitting Bull. When Catch the Bear fired at Bull Head, Bull Head then shot Sitting Bull in the ribs.

Both accounts describe an ensuing bloodbath of hand-to-hand combat that lasted for nearly an hour. E. G. Fechet, captain of the 8th Cavalry, reported that the arrest of Sitting Bull was commendable:

> *I cannot too strongly commend the splendid courage and ability which characterized the conduct of the Indian police commanded by Bull Head and Shave Head throughout the encounter. The attempt to arrest Sitting*

*Bull was so managed as to place the responsibility for
the fight that ensued upon Sitting Bull's band, which
began the firing. Red Tomahawk assumed command of
the police after both Bull Head and Shave Head had
been wounded, and it was he who, under circumstances
requiring personal courage to the highest degree, assisted
Hawk Man to escape with a message to the troops. After
the fight, no demoralization seemed to exist among
them, and they were ready and willing to cooperate
with the troops to any extent desired.*

As the sun grew higher in the December sky and turned the freezing rain into a cold drizzle, eighteen men lay dead. Sitting Bull and his son were among them.

McLaughlin described the successful arrest in his report to the United States Indian Service: "Everything is now quiet at this Agency," he penned, "and good feeling prevails among the Indians, newspaper reports to the contrary notwithstanding."

TRAGEDY AT WOUNDED KNEE: MASSACRE AND CONQUEST OF THE SIOUX

1890

The fields lay quiet as a few inches of freshly fallen snow graced the rolling prairie in south-central Dakota Territory. The frozen waters of Wounded Knee Creek were locked in dark blue ice. Covered in blankets stained with blood, Big Foot worked to build his tepee.

Big Foot's band consisted mostly of widows and their children, eager for rest along the frozen waters of Wounded Knee Creek. They had built their tepees, searched for what little food remained on the high plains, and stoked their fires to keep out the cold midwinter air. Big Foot's Lakota were not alone, as members of the Hunkpapa also camped alongside Big Foot's stand of tepees and fire rings. Rising smoke from the tepees hung in the air over the creek bottom like a thick gray blanket. The increasingly cold night air kept the warm air from rising.

Hovering just under the layer of smoke and keeping watch over the tepees were the soldiers of the 7th Cavalry. Under the command

of Colonel James Forsyth, the soldiers had met up with the Hunkpapa and Big Foot's band of Lakota and ordered them to camp along
the creek. Earlier that day the soldiers had counted the hungry and
tired Indians—120 men and 230 women and children. The soldiers
planned to disarm the Indians in the morning, taking away what
little firearms and ammunition they had.

On that cold night, with the soldiers readied for violence, it
is said that Big Foot flew a white flag of surrender and camped in
peace. Many of the Lakota and Hunkpapa were growing increasingly
ill, and some suffered from pneumonia. There was little motivation
to fight. That did not stop Forsyth from arming his 7th Cavalry
regiment with rifles, handguns, and sabers. Forsyth felt that merely
outnumbering the Indians wasn't enough, so he brought with him
several Hotchkiss guns and a powerful heavy artillery piece capable
of firing forty-three rounds per minute, and able to be transported
via mule in rough country. Forsyth knew of their use against the Nez
Perce, and felt they were necessary in Dakota Territory.

Forsyth had previously commanded the 1st Cavalry and had
overseen the command of Fort Maginnis in Montana, which encompassed the Crow, Cree, and Gros Ventre tribes. In 1886 Forsyth was
placed in command of the 7th Cavalry, where he organized a school
for field artillery and became a fan of the Hotchkiss gun. He was
familiar with this gun's power and accuracy at longer ranges, and he
wasn't afraid to use them.

As the smoke from the tepee fires grew thicker in the cooler air,
Forsyth organized his men to surround the tepees and tribal members. As Big Foot headed into his tepee for some restless sleep, the
7th Cavalry readied themselves. Their sights, and the barrels of the
Hotchkiss guns, were aimed at the tepees below.

On December 29, 1890, as the sun rose from behind the
distant hillsides, a bugle call shattered the stillness. The soldiers

ordered the men, women, and children to the center of the camp. Big Foot was escorted from his tent by a doctor. The soldiers requested that the Indians disarm themselves and bring their guns to the middle of the camp.

Not satisfied with the result, the soldiers began confiscating the few weapons the tribes possessed. As members of the 7th Cavalry demanded weapons, members of Big Foot's band and the other Lakota roiled in confusion. People were milling about as the soldiers frantically searched. The smoke cleared as the sun rose higher in the sky, only to be replaced with dust.

The search yielded only two rifles, one of which belonged to a young man named Black Coyote. Two different accounts suggest what happened next: One says Black Coyote was deaf and did not understand the soldiers' demands, while the other says he was not willing to give up his gun. Both accounts indicate that Black Coyote was proud of his weapon and had paid money for it, and was therefore reluctant to give it up without compensation.

During all of this activity, a gun fired. The source is not known. The 7th Cavalry panicked and opened fire on the hundreds of Lakota, with all the fury of the Hotchkiss guns. Because of their rapid fire, it was hard to control these guns; the soldiers showed no discretion, shooting young, old, women, and children alike. They rode miles from camp in order to shoot those who fled the scene. The soldiers even blasted women and children who were waving white flags. One witness recounted the following:

> *A mother was shot down with her infant; the child not knowing that its mother was dead was still nursing. . . . The women as they were fleeing with their babies were killed together . . . and after most of them*

had been killed a cry was made that all those who
were not killed or wounded should come forth and they
would be safe. Little boys . . . came out of their places
of refuge, and as soon as they came in sight a number
of soldiers surrounded them and butchered them there.

Another witness claims that women who were pregnant and crying out for help were gunned down, and that the bodies of women and children were found nearly three miles from camp.

When the 7th Cavalry left the creek bottom, they left nearly 350 bodies of men, women, and children in their wake, whereas only 25 soldiers were killed and 39 wounded. The few wounded Indians—4 men and 47 women and children—were placed in wagons and transported, without any medical care, to the Pine Ridge agency. Once at Pine Ridge they were left outside for hours until the Episcopal Mission opened and prepared for their arrival.

Big Foot was killed early in the tragedy, having been the target of one of the Hotchkiss guns. Because of an oncoming blizzard, all of the corpses were left in the snow and quickly froze. It would be three days before the bodies would be buried in a mass grave, on New Year's Day, without any respect paid to ceremony or burial traditions. Images of the mass grave show dozens of soldiers standing atop the bodies of the Lakota people, stacked like wood below.

Two weeks earlier, further north in Dakota Territory, Sitting Bull had been shot in a melee of gunfire on the Standing Rock Reservation. Many of the Lakota people were distraught and confused without a leader to follow. They soon confided in Big Foot, who led them from Standing Rock to the south. It was on this journey that Big Foot was confronted by the 7th Cavalry.

Big Foot and his band were seeing their lives changed forever. Because of this, many Lakota found solace in the Ghost Dance, a religion of renewal and spiritual rebirth through group dance and meditation. As their traditional lands and hunting grounds were gradually lost to homesteaders, and their main food source, the American bison, was wiped out, the Lakota were increasingly struggling with hunger and a lack of suitable homelands. The Ghost Dance religion was an escape that provided a glimmer of hope. However, Anglo settlers and U.S. government Indian Agents were afraid of the growing Ghost Dance movement, and this fear fueled an aggression toward the Lakota people that resulted in the death of Sitting Bull and the massacre at Wounded Knee.

CAPITAL COMPLEX:
MITCHELL AND PIERRE FIGHT
OVER SEAT OF GOVERNMENT

1904

Situated on the east bank of the Missouri River, in 1904 the bustling outpost of Pierre boasted a population of around 3,000. Even though it was home to the state capital, it had no *actual* capitol building. The town was served by the Chicago & Northwestern Railroad, the Missouri was a navigable waterway, and the town was a hub for South Dakota's ever-expanding western frontier.

Founded as a fur trading post, Pierre was an acceptable choice when fur trading and trapping were the reason for settlers to move into the region. In time Pierre transformed itself from a fur trading post to a military fort, and then in the early 1900s it became home to a growing livestock industry. A few fortune seekers heading into the Black Hills used Pierre as a center for their goods and services. But still the town had no physical capitol building, despite being named the capital over ten years before. South Dakotans in the eastern portion of the state thought the time was right for a capital coup.

As the eastern portion of South Dakota grew in population, some South Dakotans started to question whether it made sense to have a western capital. Many in the eastern part of the state wondered why the capital should be so far west, since the bulk of South Dakota's population lived east of the Mississippi. In fact, many felt the western portion of South Dakota was filled primarily with fortune seekers in the Black Hills, the Lakota Sioux, the 7th Cavalry, and those few trappers and traders that time had left behind. The citizens of eastern South Dakota considered themselves a much more refined and educated sort, whose livelihood was based on agriculture and goods and services, not expansion and fortune seeking.

So the fight was on as Huron, Watertown, Sioux Falls, and Mitchell all sought to be named South Dakota's state capital. Even the nonexistent town of Harrison put in a challenge to Pierre's status. Huron's challenge was short-lived. Watertown was too far north. Sioux Falls was too close to Minnesota, and Harrison never stood a chance. In 1904 Mitchell emerged as the prime candidate to challenge Pierre's ability to fairly represent South Dakotans. The citizens of Mitchell hit the campaign trail lobbying for their town and the growing interest of the more populous eastern portion of the state.

The Mitchell backers weren't afraid to sling mud or list their self-created facts. Mitchell was home to a college; Pierre was not. Mitchell bragged of elegant churches and a God-fearing people. (Although Mitchell conceded that Pierre also had churches, their structures were not as elegant, and although Pierre's citizens were religious, Mitchell felt they lacked pride in the eyes of God.) While Mitchell businesses had created a business club with 150 members, Pierre had nothing of the sort. Mitchell even went so far as to criticize Pierre for not hosting major state gatherings, noting that only minimal meetings of the state legislature had occurred in Pierre. Mitchell's citizens were sure to point out that while their town was experiencing substantial growth, Pierre was not.

Mitchell also offered to build a city hall at a cost of $55,000 and, once built, to offer a perpetual lease to the state of South Dakota until the state could erect a state capitol. Mitchell was even willing to donate land for the new capitol building.

In a letter to the voters, the citizens of Mitchell offered the following if the capital were to be transported.

> *The state may see fit to erect one of its own on a tract of land donated by the city, certainly possess a spirit of liberality that no parallel in capitol-making. It is no loss to a state to lose a home fit for little more than hats and swallows in exchange for a fireproof modern structure. No guarantee comes from Pierre as to any future improvement. Sympathy has no place in the face of a business transaction. Mitchell furnishes everything in a business way. Pierre has its natural gas only as an offering to be left alone.*

Mitchell's growth may have gone to its collective head, but there were plenty of facts in all of its boasting. In the past few years they had built more houses than any other town in South Dakota. The climate for business was ripe as local farms grew and the population expanded west due to an influx of people from Iowa, Illinois, and Minnesota. The railroad increasing their trains to more than a dozen a day also helped the economy. There was even speculation that a direct train to the Black Hills via the Milwaukee, through Chamberlain, was soon to come. Mitchell residents claimed, "Pierre can give no such promise for it has no such anticipation."

The citizens of Pierre campaigned with a little less embellishment, but their message was clear: A vote for Mitchell was a vote for state expense and increased taxes, while a vote for Pierre was a vote for state economy and relief from taxation. Pierre was not exempt from making a few low blows, however; they felt compelled to respond to Mitchell's attacks. In one campaign ad, they went on the offensive. The ad read as follows:

> *PIERRE is the corn belt, potato belt, grain belt, and fruit belt.*
>
> *And Mitchell is jealous about it.*
>
> *South Dakota is YOUR state. All of your state is* GOOD.
>
> *A VOTE FOR PIERRE is a vote for YOUR WHOLE STATE.*

Now that the two candidates were campaigning with gusto, many of the local service providers responded. Bars and hotels offered discounts to voters of one persuasion or another. Corn and grain were labeled as Pierre or Mitchell varieties. The two campaigns became so large that many citizens felt as if they were on an extended holiday. The Chicago & Northwestern Railroad offered extremely discounted rates and even some free fares; they served both Mitchell and Pierre, and their business boomed during the campaigns as visitors flocked to both towns.

Mitchell was by far the underdog, and Pierre already had the existing capital framework, despite not having a physical capitol building. Despite their best intentions and efforts, interest outside of Mitchell faded, and Pierre was able to rest assured that they would remain the capital of South Dakota—at least until the next capital challenge came.

Soon the legislature decided they should fend off any more challenges; it was time to create a permanent home for the state capitol building. In 1905 the legislature began the process that eventually led to the construction of a capitol building in Pierre.

The Mitchell challenge was not the only challenge to the capital of South Dakota, or to the Dakota Territory. In 1862 Yankton was chosen as the capital of the Dakota Territory, but in 1883, because of its central location, Bismarck (North Dakota) was chosen as capital of the territory. Later, in 1885, a constitutional convention for the territories south of the 46th Parallel was held, and Huron was named the capital. But the U.S. Congress did not recognize the 1885 Convention, so the capital remained in Bismarck.

In 1889 South Dakota achieved statehood, and Pierre was chosen as the temporary capital. In 1890 the people voted, and Pierre was chosen as the permanent site over Huron and Watertown.

TOO CORNY:
THE WORLD'S ONLY CORN PALACE

1921

The air in the gym is nearly tangible. Packed with sweaty high school kids, a few adults, and the occasional small child, the crowd sits in anticipation of the next great play. Cheerleaders frame the basketball court. Coaches eagerly pace the sidelines as the players leap for rebounds and dig in to play defense. Led by smiling cheerleaders in their short skirts, the hometown fans begin their local cheer.

"Give me a K!" the cheerleaders holler.

"K!" yells everyone in the packed stands.

"Give me an E!" "E!"

"Give me an R!" "R!"

"Give me an N!" "N!"

"Give me an E!" "E!"

"Give me an L!" "L!"

"Give me an S!" "S!"

"What's that spell?"

"Kernels!" responds the crowd.

"We can't hear you!" the cheerleaders taunt in reply.

"KERNELS!" yells the crowd.

Happy to be playing on their home court, the Mitchell High School Kernels are in for another exciting game. Like their namesake and their home court, the Corn Palace, the Kernels give the residents of Mitchell something to be oddly proud of: Mitchell is home to the world's only palace made out of corn.

Before the twentieth century Mitchell was just a sleepy farming community. Aside from a few dusty streets, typically filled with cattle and farmers trying to sell their grain, there was little reason to visit Mitchell. But a few creative business owners in Mitchell were in need of something to bring more visitors—and, eventually, more residents—to their prairie hamlet. An increased local population meant more business for the community.

It didn't take long. By 1892, these businessmen, with the help of some hardworking carpenters, built the original Mitchell Corn Palace. At the time they referred to it as the Corn Belt Exposition. The original Corn Palace was located at Fourth and Main in downtown Mitchell. In a little over ten years the Corn Belt Exposition grew, with people coming from hundreds of miles away to visit the exposition and learn about Mitchell.

In 1905 the citizens of Mitchell challenged Pierre to have the state capital of South Dakota moved to their growing farming community. The Corn Palace was one of the more intriguing locales in all of South Dakota, so the town agreed to enlarge it in an effort to increase Mitchell's appeal as a potential capital city. In time they chose to rebuild the palace altogether. The new, larger building was located just one block to the north, at Fifth and Main. The larger size also made the annual Corn Exposition that much larger, drawing even more visitors.

Even though Mitchell lost the challenge to become the capital of South Dakota, the citizens did not let their palace of corn fall into neglect. The Corn Exposition continued to grow, and by 1921, a third Corn Palace was built, just one more block to the north of the second palace. This third building, the largest of the three, was designed by the Rapp and Rapp architectural firm in Chicago.

Unique to the area, the Moorish minarets certainly stuck out among the more traditional American-style buildings typically found in Mitchell and throughout the flat prairie. However, across the United States, many buildings were incorporating Moorish Revival–style architecture into their buildings. Bulbous domes and horseshoe arches were popping up in random places, from Portland, Oregon, and Helena, Montana, to Tampa Bay, Florida, and Mitchell, South Dakota.

The architecture is one of the draws, but the main reason the Corn Palace sees over 500,000 visitors each year is because the entire exterior is covered with murals carefully created with corn kernels. The designs are created and maintained by local artists, including Oscar Howe, Calvin Schultz, and Cherie Ramsdell, among others.

Each spring the exterior is completely redone by the artist, who places a large outline of the design on the building and then fills it in with the proper-colored corn kernels. Typical themes include South Dakota Birds, A Salute to Agriculture, Youth in Action, and A Tribute to Everyday Heroes. Oftentimes the palace is referred to (in jest) as the World's Largest Bird Feeder since many birds look for fallen kernels as an easy meal. Nearly all of the corn is grown by a local farmer, Wade Strand, who plants an assortment of varieties to produce the many different colors of corn used in the murals.

The fascination with pasting corn to a building is not unique to Mitchell. Attempts at corn buildings have been made in Iowa at Sioux City and Creston. Other towns in South Dakota that have attempted palaces are Gregory and Plankinton. None of these had the staying power of the palace in Mitchell, which is truly the "World's Only" palace of corn.

The Corn Palace is now home to many local happenings, including sporting events for the local high school teams. It also serves as the home court for Dakota Wesleyan University, and many politicians have made speeches in its auditorium. Notable politicians who have graced the Palace's stage include William Howard Taft, Franklin Delano Roosevelt, Theodore Roosevelt, John F. Kennedy, Robert Kennedy, and, most recently, Barack Obama.

THE GREATEST MONUMENT NEVER FINISHED: MOUNT RUSHMORE

1927

The Lakota had long believed that the land of the Needles was sacred, and they often looked to the granite outcropping for inspiration. Located in the Black Hills, the Needles thrust from the ground as if shooting straight into the sky. They serve as a landmark to travelers, but it wasn't until one traveler passed their way that they became etched in America's history.

South Dakota's state historian, Doane Robinson, ventured into the Black Hills early in his career as historian. He knew the Black Hills were a draw for visitors, but he felt like something more could exist there. He said in a report to the legislature, "Tourists soon get fed up on scenery unless it has something of special interest connected with it to make it impressive."

Robinson soon became inspired by Stone Mountain in Georgia. In 1923 he proposed an idea: to sculpt into the Needles the forms of some of the West's great historical figures, both Native Americans and pioneers. He contacted Lorado Taft, but he was ill, so Robinson had to delay his dream. Robinson then contacted Gutzon Borglum, who was in a dispute at Stone Mountain and needed work. Borglum agreed to the project, and in his bargaining, he convinced Robinson to include George Washington and Abraham Lincoln as part of the monument.

Armed with Borglum as his artist, Robinson set out to secure funding for the project. He wanted the monument carved in Custer State Park, and asked for funds to carry out the massive sculpture. Permission was granted, as expected, but no monetary support was offered. Many Native Americans protested the construction, and a few newspapers came out against the degradation of an entire mountain.

When Borglum first visited the area, he was inspecting the Needles as a possible location, as that was Robinson's first choice. Borglum immediately found them to be too weathered and frail for his vision. After passing the Needles, Borglum and the party of supporters continued hiking through the Black Hills. As the group ventured toward Mount Rushmore, the excitement was high— would Borglum finally find a suitable mountain? Upon first glance, Borglum pointed toward the ridge and said, "America will march along the skyline."

Despite his unique name, Gutzon Borglum was born in St. Charles, Idaho. He was raised in Nebraska and then trained in Paris at the Académie Julian. Upon returning to the United States, he became a highly successful and impassioned sculptor of large-scale American monuments. His domineering, perfectionist, and authoritarian manner often brought tension to his projects, but also made it possible for him to travel the world and raise funds for much of his work, including the bulk of the fund-raising for Mount Rushmore.

The rock on Mount Rushmore was ideal for a large-scale sculpture. The mountain faces southeast and receives ample sun throughout the day. It is the highest peak of the neighboring mountains, measuring nearly 5,800 feet in elevation. The granite had only been eroding at a rate of one inch every 10,000 years—plenty of time for the monument to be enjoyed by many.

Now that Borglum had found his location, an agreement had to be made with Robinson about who would be featured on Mount Rushmore. After some heated discussions with the headstrong artist, Robinson and Borglum agreed upon George Washington, Thomas Jefferson, Theodore Roosevelt, and Abraham Lincoln.

With decisions made as to location and which personalities would appear on the mountain, and an understanding of the medium—the hard granite—Borglum set to work. He created a large-scale plaster model of the mountain and the detail of the four presidents. He used a complex method of points and measurements to scale the model to the mountain. The original plans included waist-high likenesses of the presidents.

On October 4, 1927, the first blasts were heard on the mountain. The crew blasted off the first several layers of granite until a thin layer, three to six inches, remained. The workers smoothed out the thin layer of granite, hanging by scaffolding or harnesses anchored to the top of the mountain. Once smooth, the granite had the texture of a city sidewalk.

The first feature carved into the mountain was the outline of George Washington's head, a massive egg shape. His hair, nose, eyelids, mouth, and ears would be carved later. After Washington came Thomas Jefferson. After two years of work on Jefferson's head, the granite became badly cracked. In an awesome display of exploding rock, sending granite debris flying for thousands of feet, Jefferson was blasted off the mountain. The second try was on the opposite side of Washington, his left side.

When Franklin Roosevelt was elected president, the monument was transferred to the National Park Service. At that time, a National Park Service engineer, Julian Spotts, worked side by side with Borglum.

Despite constant confrontation with the ambitious artist, Spotts was able to make many upgrades in the nature of the work. The tram carrying workers to the top of the mountain was upgraded, allowing for safer and more efficient working conditions. Spotts also worked on the air compressors to improve their ability to fire the jackhammers.

When Washington's face was finished, a large ceremony took place on July 4, 1934. Borglum, always the showman and a lover of spectacle, had several local women stitch a U.S. flag that measured 39 feet by 70 feet. He took the flag and draped it over the face of Washington. Witnesses were in tears at the sight of the massive flag. When the flag was lifted, exposing the face of the nation's first president, many tears turned into cheers.

The sculpture of Thomas Jefferson was dedicated in 1936, and President Franklin Roosevelt was in attendance. Although he was there to support the project and did not have a formal speech planned, upon seeing the monument he was moved to make the following remarks:

I had seen the photographs, I had seen the drawings, and I had talked with those who are responsible for this great work, and yet I had no conception, until about ten minutes ago, not only of its magnitude, but also its permanent beauty and importance . . . I think that we can perhaps meditate on those Americans of 10,000 years from now . . . meditate and wonder what our descendants—and I think they will still be here—will think about us. Let us hope . . . that they will believe we have honestly striven every day and generation to preserve a decent land to live in and a decent form of government to operate under.

On the 150th anniversary of the signing of the Constitution in 1937, the sculpture of Abraham Lincoln was dedicated on September 17. Two years later, on July 2, 1939, Theodore Roosevelt was dedicated. The crews had placed lights around the monument to illuminate the working areas. A large U.S. flag had been placed on Roosevelt's face, and as it was lifted, the lights slowly illuminated the night sky as hundreds of fireworks exploded over the presidents' faces.

Borglum's son Lincoln oversaw two more years of work on the mountain. During these years Gutzon Borglum worked tirelessly to raise more funds. But in March of 1941, Gutzon Borglum died due to complications from surgery while living in Chicago. The final dedication ceremony would not occur until fifty years later.

Lincoln Borglum continued to work on the project and directed it for another season of work. However, funding ran out and the monument was left as it stands today.

The monument was an ordeal from the beginning. Countless tons of granite had to be removed. When construction ceased in 1941, the total cost hovered around $900,000. If bodies were sculpted to the scale of the granite faces, they would stand 465 feet tall. The height of each face is approximately 60 feet from chin to forehead, as tall as a six-floor building. The width of an eye is 11 feet.

PARDON, MADAM: POKER ALICE SAVED FROM PRISON

1928

The air over the dusty streets of Deadwood carried the musty stench of baking horse manure. As the bright sun highlighted the lowlifes of Deadwood's bars and brothels, a short, gray-haired woman walked into one of the town's less-reputable establishments. In this saloon and gaming parlor, cattlemen sat next to horse thieves, drinking whiskey or beer—whichever the barkeep poured first. As the piano player belted out jigs, the drinks continued to flow and the poker games grew more intense. The noise of the saloon was often squelched by the rough sound of a chair being raked across the rickety floor, or by the accusations of cheating hollered across the felt tables.

But as the gray-haired woman eased her way past the swinging doors and the piano player, rested her arm on the bar and ordered a bourbon, straight up, the din of the saloon simmered down to a reasonable level. The woman took her drink, and with a steady gaze she patrolled the room, looking for the table with the highest mound of chips and the seediest characters seated around it.

Often seen with a blunt cigar protruding from her mouth, this woman was called Poker Alice. Her presence was felt not only in this saloon, but all across the West. Her birth is the subject of debate; it is often said she was born in England, although a few sources suggest she was actually born in Virginia. Alice married and eventually made her way to Deadwood, with stops along the way in New York, Colorado, New Mexico, and various points in between.

Poker Alice's adventures were no secret, as her face told of a hard life. Alice found a table, thick with cigar smoke lingering over the pile of chips, and a mix of card sharks sitting around the table like stray cats around a bowl of milk.

When Alice sat down at the table, only one of the men—Warren G. Tubbs, a gentleman down on his luck—said hello to her. The others held their poker faces. After a few hands it was clear that this woman knew how to play. None of them knew Alice had a reputation for earning as much as $6,000 a night at the tables.

Tubbs, the only man to greet Alice, soon found himself in trouble at the table. As a chair flew out from underneath one of the men, a knife was brandished, and Tubbs found himself staring down the blade, accused of cheating. Not enjoying the drama of the situation and impatient to resume playing, Alice pulled out a revolver and shot the knife-wielding man in the arm. When the dust settled, Tubbs and Alice only had eyes for each other.

Alice fell in love with Tubbs, and they soon married, had seven children, and left the life of the gambling halls for a homestead near Sturgis. Alice found that she preferred the peace and quiet of life on the ranch to playing cards in smoky saloons. She did not miss the drunks and card sharks of Deadwood. Sadly, Tubbs died of pneumonia and left Alice a widow. Heartbroken and penniless, she hired George Huckert to serve as caretaker on the ranch while she went out to gamble and earn some money. Eventually, Alice became so indebted to Huckert that she agreed to marry him, as paying him back would have cost more in the long run. Huckert died after a few years, and Alice reverted back to using Tubbs as her last name.

On her own, Alice bought a house near Bear Butte Creek, located near the Fort Meade Army Post. Seeking to provide a service to the soldiers of the post, Alice decided to create a brothel in her new home. However, her house was too small; she needed to expand, and she needed to recruit girls to work for her. She went to a local banker and convinced him to give her a $2,000 loan. Alice began work on an addition, and took a trip to Kansas City to recruit some girls. Soon, she was in business.

Alice later described her relationship with her banker:

> *I went to the bank for a $2,000 loan to build on an addition and go to Kansas City to recruit some fresh girls. When I told the banker I'd repay the loan in two years, he scratched his head for a minute, then let me have the money. In less than a year I was back in his office paying off the loan. He asked how I was able to come up with the money so fast. I took a couple chaws on the end of my cigar and told him, "Well, it's this way. I knew the Grand Army of the Republic was having an encampment here in Sturgis. And I knew that the state Elks convention would be here too. But I plumb forgot about all those Methodist preachers coming to town for a conference."*

Business was quite good, as Alice respected her working girls and had an ideal location. Despite many protests of hypocrisy,

Alice did not allow gambling or whoring on Sunday. In fact, she wasn't even open.

But unlike her good fortune at the poker table, her luck at the brothel ran out one night when a large crowd of soldiers became unruly. The house was full, the soldiers were drunk, and local law enforcement was nowhere to be found. In order to protect her girls and her house, Alice fired a rifle shot into the air to quiet the troops. Unfortunately, the bullet ricocheted, injuring one soldier and killing another.

When the police finally arrived, the soldiers fled. The brothel was closed, and Alice and all six of her girls were sent to jail. It appeared that Alice's good luck had begun to run out. However, once investigations were made into the incident, Alice and her girls were cleared of wrongdoing, as it was found that the unruly mob of soldiers had acted in a riotous manner. Despite her now-clean record, local law enforcement and the authorities at Fort Meade continued to make life difficult for Alice and her girls.

Alice was repeatedly arrested for drunkenness and domestic disorders, such as poor upkeep on her house. Alice always paid her fines in a timely manner and continued to operate her business. Even though the soldiers of Fort Meade were her main clientele, fort authorities were also her chief adversaries, and in time, they got the best of her. She was eventually arrested on a bootlegging charge, and after a quick sentencing trial, she was on her way to prison. Her luck had finally run out altogether—or had it?

Governor William John Bulow heard rumors of overzealous law enforcement in the area of Sturgis and Fort Meade. Being the first Democratic governor of South Dakota and the recipient of the highest vote ever received by a Democratic candidate, Bulow felt empowered to look into the matter. Upon meeting with Alice, Bulow quickly admitted he would be reluctant to send a white-haired lady to prison. She was pardoned and allowed to return to her home in Sturgis.

Two years later in Rapid City, Alice died following a gall bladder operation. Her house in Sturgis escaped demolition and was moved to a new location. Today, it is a bed-and-breakfast inn.

Alice was certainly a woman ahead of her time. She claimed to have won over $250,000 from gambling, and all without cheating (although she did admit to counting cards and learning the odds of every game). She was a bootlegger who owned a brothel. She was a convicted felon. She smoked cigars, had been married three times, and she'd killed a man. Poker Alice was not your typical South Dakota woman.

BURNING UP THE TRACK: "SMOKEY" JOE MENDEL WINS STATE TRACK MEET

1931

The white sport coats of the judges stood out like a sore thumb amid the bright green grass of the infield. A few young boys, rakes in hand, rushed to the long-jump pit, ready to rake out the large divot from the previous jumper. The boys raked all 22 feet and 7.5 inches of the sandy long-jump pit. Turns out they needed to rake a little more.

As the boys raked, the son of a Swiss-German Mennonite immigrant was lacing his shoes. In his head, the boy envisioned himself flying through the air and landing in the freshly raked pit. With his shoes laced and eyes focused on the takeoff line, "Smokey" Joe Mendel pumped his arms back and forth once and then fired off in a full sprint. The end of his track shoes landed on the takeoff bar perfectly. He catapulted his body into the air and flew for what seemed like minutes. When he landed, his toes were at the end of the freshly raked pit. He had covered 22 feet and 7.5 inches—a new South Dakota state record, and cause for a longer jumping pit.

Smokey Mendel was born on a farm near Freeman, South Dakota. His father, David Mendel, was the pastor at Emmanuel Krimmer Mennonite Brethren Church in Onida. Smokey was a runner and a jumper at Onida High School, and would soon prove to be one of the best.

Mendel showed his talent early. As a sophomore at Onida, he played football, but the football coach felt his running and jumping skills were so great that he needed to be part of the track and field program. At the 1924 South Dakota state track meet, Mendel won the long jump and took second place in the 100-yard dash. He also could have won the 220-yard dash, but confusion over the staggered start led Smokey to assume that he was too far behind to make up the difference.

Smokey wouldn't make the same error a year later. As a junior he won the 220-yard dash, setting a new high school record with a time of 21.7 seconds. He took second in the long jump, as well as the 100- and 440-yard dashes. In those events he lost to older athletes, who had to set state records in order to top Mendel's total score of 14 points—only one less than the winning team's total points.

Because of his performance he received an invite to participate at a prestigious national event in Chicago. At first, the Mennonite church elders said Smokey shouldn't go to the meet for fear that the participants would be too diverse. His father insisted that his son attend the meet, even against the advice of the church elders. Smokey placed fourth in the 220 and fifth in the long jump, but not without a price; the church removed him from membership.

Smokey's best feats were yet to come. As a senior at Onida, he jumped 21 feet, 9.25 inches in the preliminaries for a new state record. On a second jump he sailed 22 feet, 9.5 inches, breaking his own previously set record. In the 100-yard dash he ran a 10.0, tying the state record. In the 220-yard dash he ran a 22.1. For the

440-yard dash, his fourth and last event, Smokey faced a tough runner in Dale Palmer from Washington High School, in Sioux Falls. In the first heat, Palmer tied the state record of 51.7, but in the next heat, Smokey bested Palmer's effort and ran for a 51.2.

When the scores were tallied, Onida bested Washington by one point, winning the title, 20–19. Smokey Joe had scored all 20 of his team's points.

While at Yankton College, Smokey won the long jump and the 100- and 220-yard dashes all four years in the conference championship meets. He also matched the world-record 100-yard-dash time of 9.5 and set a state college record in 1929 with a jump of 24 feet, 1 inch. That record held for forty-five years.

Joe's high school long-jump record stood for nearly fifty years. It was broken in 1976 by Dave Bakke of Washington High School, Sioux Falls, with a leap of 23 feet, 8.25 inches. Bakke's record stood for thirty-one years, until Scott Jorgenson of Brookings sailed for 23 feet, 8.5 inches. In eighty-one years, only three people have held the boys' state long-jump record. However, the only one to single-handedly win the state track meet was Smokey Joe Mendel.

THIRSTY? WALL DRUG
SERVES SETTLERS

1931

As the rolling tumbleweeds blew across the Badlands and drifted aimlessly across the prairie, the quiet town of Wall, South Dakota, stood in the way. Not much more than a few home sites and barns back in the 1930s, Wall was home to a little over 300 people and thousands of stranded tumbleweeds. But when Nebraska native Ted Hustead and his wife Dorothy decided to purchase a piece of real estate, this sleepy prairie town would change forever.

In the early 1930s in South Dakota, most residents had been hit hard by the Great Depression. In fact, nearly all of South Dakota's rural population had suffered some form of loss, whether it was land, money, or even their lives. The Husteads were just scraping by, living in a simple apartment in Canova, South Dakota, with their four-year-old son Billy. Ted had graduated from pharmacy school in 1929 and had worked for other druggists for a couple of years. He and Dorothy felt it was time they struck out on their own.

Armed with a very small inheritance and a Model T, Ted and Dorothy and their son ventured out to find a suitable town—and drugstore—for their new adventure, during a time when many others were struggling just to get by. Their search eventually brought them to Wall, South Dakota—a town with a Catholic church, a doctor, and a banker. Everyone assured the Husteads that Wall was a town worthy of their choice, and in need of a pharmacist. Ted and Dorothy were excited and ready to start their new life.

Their parents and extended family were a little less enthusiastic, however. In their minds Wall was a busted town in the middle of the South Dakota prairie wasteland, with no redeeming qualities. They had a point: Even though the Husteads were the proud owners of a tiny drugstore, it *was* in the middle of nowhere, and they had to struggle to make ends meet in the dying prairie town. What little money there was in Wall was spent on the essentials. Few residents had proper medical care, so a visit to the drugstore was a luxury. Even with the increase in traffic from the completion of Mount Rushmore, the Husteads still found little to cheer about. Despite these obstacles, nothing was going to stop the two young entrepreneurs.

The tide would turn for them one hot summer day. Dorothy had left Ted in the store to go and take a nap, but she returned less than an hour later. Ted assumed she'd had a hard time napping because of the simmering heat outside. Dorothy said it wasn't the heat that bothered her, but the noise from all of the traffic on Route 16A. And that had given her an idea . . .

What happened next would become Wall Drug's legacy.

"Well, now, what is it that those travelers really want after driving across that hot prairie?" Dorothy asked Ted. "They're thirsty. They want water. Ice cold water! Now, we've got plenty of ice and water. Why don't we put up signs on the highway telling people to come here for free ice water? Listen, I even made up a few lines for the sign: GET A SODA . . . GET A ROOT BEER . . . TURN NEXT CORNER . . . JUST AS NEAR . . . TO HIGHWAY 16 & 14 . . . FREE ICE WATER . . . WALL DRUG."

Knowing that he'd married a smart woman, Ted got right to work on her idea. He and his son made signs, but not just typical billboards. He fashioned them after the Burma-Shave highway signs and spaced them out along the route. Each phrase would appear every so often, thus providing constant reminders of Wall Drug along the drive. Soon, FREE ICE WATER signs dotted the roads leading to and from Wall Drug. Before Ted and his son had returned to the store, travelers had already begun to visit the store. Along with their free ice water, travelers also purchased ice-cream cones, coffee, and various other goods.

After the first day of their "free ice water" promotion, Ted and Dorothy were exhausted. But as they closed up that night, enjoying the beautiful sunset from the steps of their store, a good feeling came over both of them: For the first time, they felt that buying Wall Drug had been a good decision.

The store sat on a main travel route to Mount Rushmore and Yellowstone National Park, so the constant flow of traffic was no mystery. It's still the same today; in fact, on a good summer day, Wall Drug can see as many as 20,000 visitors.

Things at Wall Drug are very different today than they were in 1931. They still offer free ice water, but the store has grown in size to nearly 50,000 square feet. The store includes a western art museum, a chapel, and an 80-foot dinosaur that is visible from Interstate 90. They offer free coffee and donuts to servicemen and -women, honeymooners, veterans, priests, hunters, truck drivers, and most other travelers. Visitors can purchase alligator boots, horse liniment, and models of Mount Rushmore and Devil's Tower. At one of the store's four cafés, the menu includes buffalo burgers. Visitors can also enjoy framed photographs of celebrities who have visited Wall Drug.

Wall Drug includes a jewelry store, two bookstores, and a shoe store with over 6,000 pairs of cowboy boots. They also have one of the nation's largest collections of jackalope mounts. The jackalope, a mythical creature that haunts the prairie, is a cross between a large jackrabbit and an antelope. Like the jackalope, Wall Drug is as unique as anyplace in the country.

Their original success was created by Dorothy's idea of roadside billboards. Today, their billboards stretch over 500 miles on I-90. They even have signs in subway stations in London and along the roadways in Paris and Rome. In Amsterdam there is a sign stating ONLY 5,397 MILES TO WALL DRUG, WALL, SD, USA. There are similar signs on nearly every continent in the world.

Even in their wildest dreams, Ted and Dorothy never could have imagined the Wall Drug of today. Their creative ideas, and the desire to give people something they want—free ice water—turned a sleepy prairie town into one of the most-talked-about locations in the U.S.

RALLY 'EM UP: THE STURGIS
MOTORCYCLE RALLY BEGINS

1938

The top of Bear Butte glistened in the morning sun. A small herd of deer grazed on the waist-high grasses near the bottom of the butte. The sleepy little Black Hills hamlet of Sturgis sat quiet as the waters of a small creek trickled through town.

An enterprising young man named J. C. "Pappy" Hoel was working in his family's business of supplying ice to the citizens in and around Sturgis. But as refrigeration became more popular and more affordable, the family business was suffering. Hoel saw little in the way of growth for the business, so he took a leap and purchased an Indian brand motorcycle store.

Indian motorcycles were the talk of the town among serious riders when Hoel began selling them. They were a small competitor to Harley-Davidson at the time and were known for the Scout and Indian Chief models. They also built an Indian Four, but that model only lasted for a few years.

Pappy Hoel found business to be good in the small town of Sturgis, and the surrounding geography proved to be an exciting place to ride. Unfortunately, he found little in the way of riding support, with no local groups of riders in the area. Pappy decided to do something about it, and, joined by a small group of enthusiastic riders, Pappy formed the Jackpine Gypsies Motorcycle Club. They joined the American Motorcycle Association and held races in their area.

The first set of organized events included a Gypsy Tour through the Black Hills. Pappy provided camping for traveling riders in his backyard, behind the Indian motorcycle dealership. Pappy's wife Pearl provided the food, eagerly serving bikers and taking care of the camping area behind their shop. Pearl handled the catering for the events with the help of a few other wives. The menu included hot dogs, sloppy joes, potato salad, and watermelon. When the hot summer sun grew intense, Pearl and Pappy set up a tent under which to serve the growing crowds. Riders from all over came to enjoy the camaraderie and to sample Pearl's cooking.

Eventually, Pappy was able to join with the city of Sturgis to create a half mile of dirt track. The Black Hills Gypsy Tour was followed up by a single race on the newly created track. The first race had nine racers, and the audience was small but excited. There were a few more races held on the dirt track that first year, and biker "Smiling" Johnny Spiegelhoff brought home most of the glory.

In the heat of early August, 1939, what had begun a year before as an informal gathering of motorcycle enthusiasts blossomed into a full-fledged rally, with over 800 riders. Pappy and Pearl's electric personalities and reputation for providing great hospitality proved to be a great draw. Nineteen riders participated in the first rally, which included the half-mile track racing, board wall crashes, ramp jumps, and head-on collisions with automobiles.

Soon the Jackpine Gypsies were operating the tracks, the hillclimbs, and the large field areas. Stunts and racing were the primary events of the first few rallies, and many of the riders became celebrities in motorcycle circles across the country. The Black Hills Motorcycle Classic was born.

By the 1940s the rally was truly a spectator sport. On average over 5,000 people attended each rally. In 1947 over 400 riders participated in the Jackpine Gypsy tour, with the Gypsies still providing most of the labor and logistical support for the rallies. The Jackpine Gypsies gradually purchased additional land to use in their races. They leased a hill east of Sturgis, as well as a hill near Bear Butte's south side, for hillclimbs. They raised money and even built a little clubhouse. During this time they saved money from entry fees and various fund-raisers, and eventually had enough money to purchase 30 acres for a hillclimb, a motocross track, and a short track. These 30 acres also include the current tracks, near Short Track Road.

For the next thirty years the rally continued to grow. By the mid-1980s it was bringing over 30,000 people to Sturgis. Pappy created a monument that sits along Junction Avenue today, listing the fastest riders from the annual races. In 1985 Governor Bill Janklow signed a proclamation declaring the annual week of the rally "Pappy Hoel Week." In 1985, many events at the rally commemorated Pappy and his founding vision.

By the 1990s the rally had become too large for the Jackpine Gypsies to handle. Sturgis Rally and Races, Inc. was formed to handle the promotion, planning, and security of the event. In 1992, after an extensive process, Sturgis Rally and Races, Inc. changed the name from Black Hills Motorcycle Classic to the Sturgis Rally and Races. Since that time events have spilled over into other areas of the Black Hills.

Today, the event has become more of a family affair. Some riders don't like the change, saying that the focus has shifted away from the races and the skills of the riders and more toward concerts and games. But the spirit of Pappy and Pearl can still be felt in the friendliness of the residents and the wide array of attendees—from parents with kids to full-time bikers.

The rallies had their own celebrity image in the 1990s: In 1997 the television show *Cops* had an on-the-ground crew. Dennis Rodman made an appearance at the rally. The previous year, World Championship Wrestling hosted a pay-per-view event, titled *Hog Wild*. More recently, ESPN featured the rallies in their *50 States in 50 Days* feature.

Attendance has skyrocketed in recent years; in 2004 and 2005, over 500,000 people were estimated to have attended the rally. In 2000, attendance was estimated at over 750,000. The 2000 event was deemed the largest-ever outdoor event in the United States.

For most of August the air in Sturgis is full of dust and motorcycle fumes. Pappy and Pearl Hoel would be proud.

TRULY GREAT BADLANDS: PRESIDENT ROOSEVELT CREATES BADLANDS NATIONAL MONUMENT

1939

Dust blew heavy across the high plains of western South Dakota. As homesteaders and ranchers struggled to find a way to make a living, bureaucrats in government offices scratched their heads, asking why the Great Depression had hit them so hard. After fighting off drought, crop failures, and grasshopper outbreaks, a few driven individuals took on the mission of establishing a park in the Badlands of South Dakota.

Ben Millard, owner of Cedar Pass Lodge; A. G. Granger of Kadoka; Leonel Jensen, a local rancher; Ted Hustead, owner of Wall Drug; and Dr. G. W. Mills of Wall felt that the area south of their homes was like no place else on earth. Jagged hilltops carved from thousands of years of wind and rain protruded from the earth. Fossils buried deep in the ground had become exposed as the loose soil eroded away. Creeks flowed in the coulees. Deer and antelope grazed the native grasses. Like a blister on a clean face, the Badlands stood in stark contrast to the normally flat and nondescript high plains of western South Dakota.

These men shared a vision of showcasing the wonders of the Badlands. Millard worked to acquire federal lands in the area of the Badlands. He, along with one of his employees, worked with the U.S. government to set the route for the alternate U.S. Highway 16. He later agreed to donate vital pieces of his land to the government to be included in the monument.

Because of the Great Depression and its impact on the rural areas of South Dakota, the federal government sought to assist people in hard-hit areas. The area around the Badlands was one of the hardest hit. Because of the government programs and the location of the Badlands, the National Park Service (NPS) was able to obtain land quite easily. The NPS wanted to expand the monument for many reasons; one of the main reasons was to assist area farmers and ranchers with compensation for their lands. But in order to do so, the NPS had to obtain both authorization and funding.

The NPS asked for three things: First, that the president be allowed to issue an executive order removing all public lands from the proposed monument area; second, that all privately owned lands be acquired through a federal relief program; and third, that Congress be asked to establish the Badlands National Monument.

Less than three weeks after the NPS request, President Franklin D. Roosevelt issued the following order for lands in Pennington, Jackson, Fall River, and Custer counties:

> [That these lands be] temporarily withdrawn from settlement, location, sale, or entry, for classification and use as a grazing project pursuant to the submarginal land program of the Federal Emergency Relief Administration [FERA].

This executive order set in place the framework for the Badlands National Monument. The NPS then acquired over 20,000 acres of private land lying within the proposed monument. Soon the NPS sought further lands and gained the support of South Dakota governor Tom Berry, Senator Peter Norbeck, President C. C. O'Hara of the South Dakota School of Mines, and many other prominent natural historians and educators.

But it was a letter from Secretary of the Interior T. A. Walters that cemented the federal government's desire to obtain the lands and work to ease the financial hardships facing the region:

> *I hereby recommend for purchase certain lands for a project known as the Badlands National Monument Extension in Jackson, Pennington, Washington and Washabaugh Counties, South Dakota, proposed by the National Park Service of this Department for the conservation and development of the natural resources of the United States, within the meaning of Section 202 of Title II of the National Industrial Recovery Act, pursuant to which funds have been allotted and transferred to the Land Program, Federal Emergency Relief Administration.*

In order to obtain funding to expand the monument and pay landowners, Walters recommended to President Roosevelt that the monument extension project be funneled into the Recreational Demonstration Project of FERA's Land Program. Much of the lands, however, would be in various states of use and non-use, as described by Senator Norbeck in a letter to the NPS:

A very large percentage of this land, maybe 30 to 50 percent, is on the tax delinquency list, with about four years of taxes. The price offered is less than the taxes held against the land, and the owner is not anxious to sell if he cannot get a nickel out of it. . . . Considerable of these lands, however, have already been abandoned by the owner on account of the amount of taxes due.

At the time, counties did not want to sell land to the federal government, as they lost tax revenue. However, many farmers and ranchers were unable to pay the taxes, and many even desired to sell their land—for whatever price they could get. One desperate letter from the wife of a local rancher stated the following:

After six years [of] crop failures on the so-called submarginal land of Western South Dakota, we are facing financial disaster unless we sell our land to the government.

Knowing that much of his constituency was struggling this way, Norbeck lobbied the federal government to increase their offering price by one dollar an acre—an increase on the average price, which was $2.85 an acre. The request was granted. Norbeck then worked to gain the support of various farm relief agencies, to build roads in the area, and to contract for buildings, infrastructure, and other uses.

Congress approved the request of the NPS for the boundary extension and creation of the national monument—but not until Governor Berry urged the NPS to have a formal presidential proclamation. The provisions of Public Law 1021 had been met—the highway was built, and the state had acquired the privately owned lands. The total acreage owned by the federal government included a little over 110,000 acres, and there were about 40,000 acres of state-owned lands.

Despite the convoluted route that had been taken, on January 25, 1939, President Roosevelt formally created the Badlands National Monument. It became the 77th national monument and the 151st area in the federal park system.

In 1978 the monument was reestablished at Badlands National Park. Since its creation as a national monument in the early twentieth century, the lands have been used in various ways—from grazing for cattle to a World War II gunnery range. In 1976 the Oglala Sioux agreed to comanage some of the lands. This agreement added the Stronghold and Palmer Creek units.

Today the park is nearly 244,000 acres in size and is home to the largest protected native grass prairie in the United States, with 64,000 acres designated as wilderness. It is the site of the reintroduction of the black-footed ferret. The Oglala Sioux have protected areas in the Stronghold Unit where many of the Ghost Dances occurred in the late nineteenth century.

The park's geology is remarkable. It contains one of the world's richest fossil beds, which is between 23 and 35 million years old. Numerous fossils have been found, from squid-like creatures to giant lizards, from pterosaurs to water-diving birds. Fossils of saber-toothed cats have been found, as well as those of a distant relative of the rhinoceros.

Perhaps architect Frank Lloyd Wright best described the Badlands with the following quote:

I've been about the world a lot, and pretty much over our own country, but I was totally unprepared for that revelation called the Dakota Bad Lands. . . . What I saw gave me an indescribable sense of mysterious elsewhere—a distant architecture, ethereal . . . an endless supernatural world more spiritual than earth but created out of it.

A MOUNTAIN OF A MONUMENT: CRAZY HORSE MEMORIAL

1948

Fireworks and fanfare engulfed the foot of Mount Rushmore. As the red and blue blasts illuminated the faces of George Washington, Abraham Lincoln, Thomas Jefferson, and Teddy Roosevelt, ambitious sculptor Korczak Ziolkowski looked upon the colossal monument he had helped to create.

Ziolkowski was orphaned at birth and grew up in a series of foster homes in Boston. After putting himself through school and working as an apprentice for a Boston shipbuilder, Ziolkowski made his first sculpture. He slowly gained notoriety as an artist, and even won a first prize at the New York World's Fair. He moved west to work on Mount Rushmore, and soon, his notoriety and familiarity with the Black Hills sparked the interest of Chief Henry Standing Bear of the Lakota.

Chief Standing Bear composed a simple letter to Ziolkowski: "My fellow chiefs and I would like the white man to know the red man has great heroes, too." That was all Ziolkowski needed to begin work on his newest project.

Ziolkowski began his search for a suitable mountain. He originally wanted to carve the monument in the Tetons of Wyoming, but the Lakota wanted the monument to be located in the Black Hills. After consulting with the tribe, construction began on Thunderhead Mountain, more than 600 feet higher than most other mountains in the area.

Just as Thunderhead Mountain was unique, so was the relationship between Ziolkowski and Crazy Horse, the subject of his newest sculpture. Crazy Horse was killed exactly thirty-one years before Ziolkowski was born. Then, thirty-one years after that, Standing Bear wrote to Ziolkowski.

Crazy Horse used to wear a small stone in his ear. When others asked about the stone, he would respond, "I will return to you in the stone." When Crazy Horse's friend Black Elk told this story to Ziolkowski, the words were etched in the sculptor's memory for good.

Originally, Standing Bear and Ziolkowski agreed to a 100-foot carving atop Thunderhead Mountain. Eventually, however, Ziolkowski grew more ambitious, and felt that a mountaintop carving was not enough. He wanted a larger sculpture. His new plans called for this monument to be the largest sculpture in the world. When finished, it would be over 560 feet high and over 640 feet long. The head of Crazy Horse would be nearly 90 feet high—large enough to contain all four heads of the presidents on Mount Rushmore. The outstretched arm would be over 260 feet long. The head of the horse would be over 200 feet high. Crazy Horse's finger alone would be nearly 40 feet long and 10 feet thick, and his hand, over 30 feet thick.

The sculpture would depict Crazy Horse riding a horse and pointing outward, over the mane of the horse. This pose is interpreted to mean "My lands are where my dead lie buried," the statement Crazy Horse supposedly uttered when he was asked, "Where are your lands now?"

When the first blasts were made into the mountain, a memorial service was held, dedicating the monument to Native Americans. Ziolkowski chose Crazy Horse as the subject of his work to honor the fallen Sioux warrior and chief. This project would prove to be a challenge, however, as Crazy Horse had never allowed his picture to be taken. Much of Crazy Horse's history is shrouded in mystery and controversy. Along with his likeness, the facts surrounding his death are also largely unconfirmed.

While various accounts all say that Crazy Horse died after being treated for stab wounds by Dr. Valentine McGillycuddy at Fort Robinson, no conclusive evidence exists regarding who stabbed Crazy Horse, and why. What follows is a widely published account of Crazy Horse's last few words:

> *After that I went up on the Tongue River with a few of my people and lived in peace. But the government would not let me alone. Finally, I came back to the Red Cloud Agency. Yet, I was not allowed to remain quiet. I was tired of fighting. I went to the Spotted Tail Agency and asked that chief and his agent to let me live there in peace. I came here with the agent [Lee] to talk with the Big White Chief but was not given a chance. They tried to confine me. I tried to escape, and a soldier ran his bayonet into me. I have spoken.*

Dr. McGillycuddy expressed doubt about whether Crazy Horse had ever been photographed. Historian Walter Camp, in doing research, asked the agent at Pine Ridge Indian Reservation for a photo of Crazy Horse. The agent replied: "I have never seen a photo of Crazy Horse. Nor am I able to find any one among our Sioux here who remembers having seen a picture of him. Crazy Horse had left the hostiles but a short time before he was killed and it's more than likely he never had a picture taken of himself."

There remains one disputed image, but most historians agree the image is not of Crazy Horse. A few others surfaced over time, but the consensus among scholars is that they are not photographs of Crazy Horse.

In response to questions and doubts about Crazy Horse's life and death, Ziolkowski responded by saying the sculpture is an envisioned response to the spirit of Crazy Horse. He never intended to represent the exact image of Crazy Horse. Ziolkowski chose Crazy Horse because he felt Crazy Horse was a great hero. He admired Crazy Horse's purpose, his simple life, and his courage, and he wanted to honor Crazy Horse's tragic death. Crazy Horse showed great loyalty to his people, and his personal values expressed concern for his elders, the widowed, and young children. Ziolkowski clearly felt great respect for Crazy Horse and offered the following statement when questioned about carving someone who didn't want to be photographed: "Crazy Horse is being carved not so much as a lineal likeness but more as a memorial to the spirit of Crazy Horse—to his people."

Despite controversy, Ziolkowski persevered and denied any federal funding. He was afraid that if he took any money from the government, they would have had the power to alter his original vision for the monument, which was to honor Crazy Horse and all Native Americans. He was offered $10 million on two occasions, but refused. He wanted individuality and private enterprise to reign supreme over government involvement. He felt it was more important to ensure that his long-range goal of honoring Crazy Horse would be guaranteed rather than simply fulfilling the short-term goal of having the money to complete the memorial.

Ziolkowski continued to work on the massive memorial project, joined by his wife Ruth and their children, but he died in 1982 before the monument was completed. Today the mountain and visitor center are owned by the Crazy Horse Memorial Foundation, which works tirelessly to uphold Ziolkowski's original mission and to secure funding for the memorial's completion. The foundation sponsors many Native American cultural events and educational programs. Much of the major work on the memorial is done with equipment donated by businesses. Over one million people visit the memorial each year.

POWER PLAY: OAHE DAM
IS COMPLETED

1962

The waters of "Old Misery" sparkled in the morning sunshine. The blowing wind of the South Dakota plains took a break as children ran from their yards. Adults gossiped back and forth about the town's special visitor. The dignitaries and officers were lined up and seated, brimming with admiration and anticipation. As the calm waters of the Missouri River lay quiet, the town of Pierre was buzzing.

A large grandstand had been built, and rows of seats were filled with excited onlookers. Members of the Secret Service surveyed the scene. As the crowd rose, President John F. Kennedy made his way to the podium, glistening with the presidential seal. Addressing the crowd of South Dakotans, the president offered gratitude for their hard work. On this day, August 17, 1962, the world's largest rolled-earth dam, the Oahe, had finally been completed. Kennedy knew it had been no small feat, and not without great sacrifice.

Before the dam was created, each spring the wide Missouri River would rise and drop with melting snow and heavy rains. The towns of Pierre and Yankton were annual victims of floods. After typical heavy, wet, spring snows, the Missouri would often rise over its banks, wreaking havoc on the small farming communities. The river soon became known as "Old Misery" because of its unruly behavior.

As if wide-scale flooding wasn't enough, the entire region had also been hit hard by the Great Depression. As the region sought to claw itself back to normalcy, the constant flooding was a reminder that life on the prairies of South Dakota was not easy. Even when Lewis and Clark had passed this way in 1804, they had noted the amount of flooding that occurred here.

The U.S. Congress felt something needed to be done. The Flood Control Act created legislation that would allow for the construction of dams along the entire length of the Missouri. Despite its good intentions, the law came with a high price, making it acceptable to transfer massive parcels of land around the Missouri River to the federal government. More than one-fifth of the lands along the entire Missouri River system used to be owned by Native Americans or were part of Indian reservations.

Despite receiving compensation, many of the reservations and tribes lost substantial, and vital, tracts of land. The Lakota, Dakota, and Nakota tribes lost a total of 202,000 acres. Near the Fort Berthold Reservation, the Mandan, Hidatsa, and Arikara tribes lost 155,000 acres. The Oahe Dam saw the Cheyenne River Indian Reservation lose 150,000 acres of land. The Standing Rock Reservation lost 55,990 acres. Most of the lands along the Missouri River were prime agricultural lands. In the transfer of land, the two reservations lost much of their best farmland. In one instance, when asked by a visitor why there were very few older Indians, a tribal elder responded, "The old people died of heartache." He was referring to the construction of the dam and the loss of reservation lands.

Native Americans were not the only people displaced by the Flood Control Act and by the building of the Oahe Dam. A few towns were relocated, and some were even abandoned.

The town of Pollock had roots dating back to 1901. It began as a railroad town, but when the Oahe Dam was being constructed, the town had to make a tough choice: to either move or to disband. The townspeople met and voted to move a mile to the south. Many of the town's citizens built new homes and businesses, but a few stubborn folks moved buildings to the new town site. Today, Pollock is home to about 500 people, and the river is a large part of daily life, providing water for farms and recreation.

Having successfully moved people and property out of the way of imminent flooding, the Army Corps of Engineers could get to work. They began moving large amounts of earth to create a massive dirt embankment. Once they had moved most of the dirt, they drilled large sheet pilings (interlocking panels) to keep the water from seeping out under the embankment. Since they were still working on the embankment, they didn't want it to fill yet. In order to prevent it from filling, they had to create six massive tunnels under the dam.

These outlet tunnels allowed water to flow under the dam before the dam was fully completed. The tunnels are 19 feet in diameter, and the tunnels leading to the powerhouses are 24 feet in diameter. Much of the equipment brought in to build the tunnels and create the embankment—at the time, some of the largest of its kind in the entire world—was custom-built for the project.

Once the earthen embankment was completed, they closed off the outlet tunnels and the lake began to rise, creating Lake Oahe. While they were working on the embankment, construction also began on seven powerhouses, which would house the generators. The first generator began producing power the same year that President Kennedy appeared in Pierre and dedicated the dam.

The dam is 245 feet high, and the volume of earth used in the embankment, which stretches for 9,300 feet, was 92,000,000 cubic yards. The volume of cement used was 1,122,000 cubic yards. The lake is 205 feet deep and can store 2.35 million acre-feet of water. The total cost of the project was $340,000,000.

The public takes advantage of the shoreline's fifty-one recreation sites. The lake is long and narrow because it has filled an old riverbed, not a large valley. It stretches for over 230 miles, into North Dakota.

Today the dam employs hundreds of people. The fishing and waterfowl hunting on the lake is some of the best in the state. The water storage gives farmers and ranchers consistent access to irrigation water. And, despite the loss of many Native American sites, the 2,400 miles of shoreline still honors the state's history and culture. One such place is the Huff Archaeological Site, a former fortified village of the Mandan, located in North Dakota. Unfortunately, this site is currently at risk of being eroded by Lake Oahe.

SHAKY YEAR: THE EARTHQUAKES OF 1964

The morning of March 23, 1964, was like most other mornings in southwestern South Dakota. Farmers worked in their fields, children waited for the school bus, and office workers spent the morning discussing things over the watercooler. The day passed as any other, and as the sun set beyond the Black Hills, night fell upon the arid landscape of the plains.

As the clock struck midnight and a new day began, most folks were asleep in their beds. But, as the minutes passed and sleepers snored, that would soon change. At 12:12 a.m., the earth shook. And shook some more. Buildings rattled, books fell off the shelves, and people awoke from their sleep. For almost five seconds the ground shook as a tremor rattled southwestern South Dakota.

The quake's center was pinpointed in Custer County, near Hot Springs and the Fall River–Custer County border. The towns of Keystone, Pine Ridge, and Provo all reported movement. In nearby Van Tassell, Wyoming, witnesses reported dishes falling out of cabinets and broken shelving. In Harrison and Hyannis, Nebraska, a few buildings received cracks in their foundations.

In Wind Cave National Park, a little north of the center of the quake, rocks rattled in the cave and fell from above. The noise from the falling rocks would have been quite loud, but at midnight no witnesses were around to report any noise—only damage that was discovered later in the day on March 24.

As the sun rose on the 24th, citizens were relieved that the quake had been relatively small; however, with a rating of around 5 in intensity, it had still created enough movement to wake people from their beds.

As people relaxed from the excitement of the quake and went about their day, no other quakes were felt. For the next three nights, things were uneventful for most people in the region. But at 9:00 p.m. on the night of March 27, the region shook again. As people were enjoying an evening in front of the television or having a late dinner at the kitchen table, books shook and dishes rattled. Fortunately, no widespread damage occurred. The center of this aftershock was believed to be closer to Wyoming, but the citizens of southwestern South Dakota still felt the movement.

The rating of this second quake was never measured, as a large earthquake in Alaska disrupted any measurements. Despite scientists assuring local citizens, many felt that the shaking from the quake on March 27 was a result of the massive earthquake in Alaska, although no connection between the two has ever been proven.

News of the quakes quickly spread across South Dakota. Excitement and nervousness were high across the state, and it didn't take long before another region was rocked by earthquakes. Only a day passed before a magnitude 5.1 quake shook south-central South Dakota for nearly 10 seconds, on March 28, 1964. Although the center was placed near Merriman, Nebraska, less than 15 miles across the border, houses and everything in them shook for about five seconds. Highways cracked, steep banks eroded into rivers and onto roads, and general mayhem ruled for a fraction of a minute. If it hadn't been for the timing of the quake, at shortly after 3:00 a.m., the quake could have caused many severe injuries.

In South Dakota, dishes were reported broken in many homes. Several homeowners also reported broken stucco under window frames. In Deadwood, on the other side of the Black Hills, a retaining wall was damaged. In Interior, South Dakota, the plaster on ceilings cracked and fell to the ground. At Martin, the closest town to the center of the quake, a glass storage container shattered and sent shards of glass flying in all directions. In Pine Ridge, widespread ceiling damage was also reported.

The quake was registered in parts of Wyoming, Montana, and Nebraska. Residents of Alzada, Montana, over 150 miles away, reported damage from the quake. The entire area affected by the quake measured 230,000 square kilometers.

For the next three years minor quakes rattled southwestern South Dakota. In June of 1966 a quake damaged a patio and concrete steps in Rapid City. Well waters were contaminated at Keystone. A tree fell in Deadwood because of the quake. This quake was a 4.1 magnitude, and effects were felt in Silver City, Black Hawk, Hill City, Lead, Piedmont, Pine Ridge, and Shannon.

On November 23, 1967, a magnitude 4.4 quake shocked the region. Houses shook and dishes tumbled off shelves in Winner, Rosebud, and White River. In Gregory residents reported furniture sliding across the floor and windows cracking. Reports of livestock stampeding were also rampant. This quake was also felt in Carter, Chamberlain, Colome, Martin, Mission, and Stephan. Parts of Nebraska and Wyoming also felt shocks.

It would be four years until the next earthquake occurred between Kadoka and Norris in 1971.

The most recent earthquake in South Dakota occurred in February of 2007. It was a small quake, only measuring 3.1 in magnitude. The quake was most likely ignored by all, as it occurred at 3:36 a.m. The center was near Wall.

South Dakota averages a few earthquakes every two to three years. The southern half of the state, and especially the southwestern corner, are the most active regions. Since 1900, the state has recorded as many as sixty-five earthquakes.

BLACK HILLS RUN BROWN: THE RAPID CITY FLOOD

1972

June 9, 1972, was shaping up to be a typical early summer Friday night in Rapid City. High school kids were ready for the summer, enjoying shakes and burgers at a local drive-in. Ranchers had finished their chores early, and families were planning an enjoyable weekend of exploring the Black Hills.

Rain had been falling in the Black Hills for most of the work week, but that wasn't about to stop anyone from enjoying a pleasant weekend. Even as the horizon grew darker and the hills west of Rapid City were swallowed by heavy clouds, people packed campers, sat in their yards, and rested from a busy week. But for the next six hours, the rain in the nearby hills never let up; in fact, it would prove fatal.

As the dark clouds parked over the eastern edge of the Black Hills, the winds died down, the air cooled, and the rain poured. And poured some more. The clouds did not move and the rain kept falling. In the next four hours, record rainfall amounts of between 4 to 12 inches were recorded in the Rapid Creek watershed. In the Box Elder Creek watershed near Nemo, 15 inches of rain fell in six hours.

Another location reported 4 inches in thirty minutes. The heaviest rainfall averaged about four times the six-hour amounts that are expected once every 100 years in the area.

Nearly every creek draining the mountains west of Rapid City leapt its banks as water rushed into fields, over bridges, and took with it bankside vegetation, creating a muddy torrent of cold water.

But at the foothills of the Black Hills, the citizens of Rapid City were too busy planning their weekend, and they were unaware of what was to come. The ground oozed with rainwater, and Rapid Creek became higher and higher.

The National Weather Service had alerted the Rapid City Police Department and the Pennington County sheriffs of the potential for grave danger from the rising waters of Rapid Creek. But by the time police officers and deputies began alerting local officials and residents, large logs, boulders, and even cars were being carried by the brown waves of the raging creek. On Rapid Creek upstream of Canyon Lake, a bridge below a state fish hatchery was wiped out by a full-size sedan being carried in the rush of waters.

For the time being, the Canyon Lake Dam was still protecting the citizens of Rapid City from the surging waters.

Higher in the Black Hills, a small dam upstream of Rapid City, Pactola Reservoir, was holding under the runoff, but most of the rain was falling in the drainages downstream of Pactola. It was the dam on Canyon Lake that most worried the weather service and emergency officials. Above Canyon Lake, Rapid Creek rose 13 feet in five hours. As the runoff from Rapid Creek pounded Canyon Lake Dam and exploded over the spillway, it carried floating logs, a few cars, and other debris. The massive amount of debris slowly clogged the spillway of the dam, creating a ticking time bomb of logs, cars, metal, and raging waters. All that stood between the residents of Rapid City and the surging water was the Canyon Lake Dam—and Rapid Creek kept rising.

Shortly after 7:00 p.m., as the debris continued to pile up in the Canyon Lake Dam spillway, Rapid City mayor Don Barnett and Rapid City public works director, Leonard Swanson, drove from Rapid City to the dam. Their mission was to force the caretaker to move his family from their house, which was located just below the dam. Barnett and Swanson ordered them to leave their meal on the dining room table and get out immediately. A few hours later, around 10:45 p.m., the Canyon Lake Dam failed and nearly 50,000 cubic feet of water rushed through the broken dam, headed on a path of destruction toward Rapid City.

As the clock ticked toward midnight, many residents of Rapid City were asleep and unaware of the raging waters headed their way. Although radio and television stations had been broadcasting warnings nonstop, a massive power outage occurred, and the stations were unable to continue. They would not return to the airwaves until morning.

The waters of Rapid Creek ravaged the town of Rapid City from midnight until early Saturday morning. During that time, pickup trucks, street signs, trees, steel, and mud caromed through downtown Rapid City, leaving behind a path of carnage. By 5:00 a.m. Rapid Creek was back in it banks as the waters eventually ran into the Cheyenne River, leaving Rapid City in a turmoil of water, mud, and destruction. The nightmare was over.

During the night, Frank Parker, owner of Marv's Wrecker Service, worked to rescue many people trapped in the fury. When the floodwaters became too high, he clung to a telephone pole for safety for nearly four hours. Fires from exploding gas lines lit up the night sky as Parker held on for dear life most of the night. He was eventually rescued without any major injuries.

The American Red Cross set up refuge areas for drinking water and provided inoculations for rescue workers and for people injured during the night.

Despite the fact that the tragedy had lasted less than eight hours—the Canyon Lake Dam had failed around 10:45 p.m. and Rapid Creek had returned to its banks by 5:00 a.m.—residents would not grasp the scope of the disaster until the waters had settled.

Frank Parker's towing business alone had hauled thousands of damaged automobiles out of the carnage of Rapid City. But the damage to automobiles was nothing compared to the loss of life caused by the disaster. The American Red Cross reported 238 deaths and 5 missing people. Of the 238 dead, 3 were National Guardsmen; 3 were firefighters; 7 were Air Force officers; and 1 was a reserve police officer. Over 3,000 people were injured and 118 were hospitalized.

The toll of destruction on real estate was just as astonishing: 770 permanent homes and 565 mobile homes were destroyed, while 2,035 permanent homes and 785 mobile homes were damaged. Thirty-six businesses were wiped out entirely, while over 230 were damaged. Over 5,000 vehicles were destroyed.

In Rapid City over $65 million in residential and commercial damage occurred. In the area around Rapid City, $10 million in utilities and $35.4 million in roads and bridges were lost, while an estimated $30 million of tourism dollars were lost. The total damages exceeded $165 million throughout the Black Hills—nearly $700 million in today's dollars.

Despite the tragedy, the citizens of Rapid City united and created a park and a memorial to the victims of the flood, located in the middle of town.

The flood was not without its lighter side. Shortly after the terrible tragedy, a rumor was floating around that the crocodiles from Reptile Gardens, a nearby tourist attraction, had escaped during the flood and were roaming the area. Fortunately, as if nearly $200 million in damages and a death toll of 238 people were not enough, there were no crocodiles at large in Rapid City.

REINJURED: WOUNDED KNEE II

1973

The dark gray sky hung over the empty plains of south-central South Dakota. A small dusting of snow lay on the ground, barely covering the grasses, brown and yellow in their midwinter dormancy. There were very few signs of life on the plains this February day.

Protected from the elements, members of the American Indian Movement (AIM) and the local Oglala Lakota Sioux were contemplating their future inside their homes on the Pine Ridge Indian Reservation. For nearly a hundred years the Sioux had been struggling with the settlement of non-Indians. The U.S. government had made—and broken—treaties and created development that resulted in the Native Americans losing their tribal lands. Because of many of these past actions, along with current issues like poverty, high unemployment, and police brutality, the nonviolent American Indian Movement had been created. It was a movement of action and principle, but as tensions increased, the movement began to monitor and protest police activities. They felt an aggressive stance was necessary in order for the voices of many neglected people to be heard. Until the winter of 1973, the voices of Native Americans in the U.S. had been largely unheard and ignored.

As the dark, gray sky hung overhead, the Pine Ridge Indian Reservation felt the weight of many burdens. Many of the Lakota living on the reservation believed their lands had been stolen. Many still felt the Black Hills should be returned to them, according to promises made in government treaties. Their current lands were also being destroyed by nearby strip mines. Many people on the reservation were becoming sick, children were suffering birth defects, and the land was looking less like traditional Sioux lands. Many on the reservation felt the effects of the strip mines were causing these health problems.

A small division grew among members of the Oglala Sioux, which led to the opposition of tribal chairman Richard A. "Dick" Wilson. Members who opposed Wilson accused him of mishandling tribal funds, abusing authority, and ignoring the decisions of the tribal council. They asked members of AIM for assistance. The main founders of AIM—Clyde Bellecourt and Dennis Banks, Chippewa from Minnesota—were interested. Russell Means, an Oglala Sioux, would become one of the more prominent members of AIM and a key player in what was to happen at Pine Ridge.

As members of AIM arrived on the reservation, the interests and concerns of the U.S. government were ignited. Government officials had been monitoring AIM ever since the movement had taken over the Bureau of Indian Affairs (BIA) building in Washington, D.C., for almost a week in November of 1972. AIM had sought to negotiate with the federal government for better housing and other issues as part of their Trail of Broken Treaties.

When AIM descended upon Pine Ridge in 1973, the U.S. Department of Justice followed. They sent U.S. Marshals to the reservation and ordered them to monitor the scene in case civil violence were to ensue. Even though tensions were already high, there was an eerie sense of calm. That would quickly change.

As members of the reservation confided in AIM and asked members to help them oust Wilson, the fifty U.S. Marshals on hire by the U.S. government stood watch, monitoring the movements of people and goods in and out of Pine Ridge. AIM's goals were to reform the tribal government and bring to light Native American grievances. They asked Congress to investigate the conditions on all Indian reservations, as well as alleged corruption in the BIA.

The details of the next seventy-one days are hazy, as AIM and the U.S. government offer differing accounts. AIM claimed they were in the area to assist concerned members in the abuses of tribal chairman Wilson. Their meetings were open to all, and violence was purposefully left out of any equation. However, as AIM met with tribal members on the morning of February 27, 1973, they claimed that the FBI and the U.S. Marshals were beginning to quarantine them by setting up roadblocks and restricting access to the town.

The U.S. government officials in the area claimed they were there to prevent injury or death and to ensure that no one violated any laws. They said it was necessary to restrict the supply of weapons and ammunition to members of AIM. In setting up barricades and roadblocks in and out of the town and Pine Ridge, they restricted the movements of families and friends.

The White House, the Department of Defense, and the Department of Justice worked together to create a military presence. They brought in the personnel, weapons, and equipment necessary to deal with an armed conflict. A feeling of violence moved into the area and tensions soon reached the boiling point.

For the next two months both sides traded gunfire. People struggled through hidden trenches and fought the elements to bring essential things like food and water to people living in Pine Ridge. Electricity was shut off to most of the town.

To justify their actions of blockades, military force, and quarantine, the U.S. government claimed that AIM had taken hostages, and that officials were there to demand their release. AIM claimed that their occupation of Pine Ridge was requested and justified.

Senators James Abourezk and George McGovern arrived at Wounded Knee shortly after the standoff began, hoping to negotiate with members of AIM. It is said they were able to talk with Russell Means, and they all agreed to some conditions. Abourezk and McGovern returned to Washington, D.C., assuring AIM leaders that there would be some resolution. But the U.S. government officials on the ground chose to stay; in fact, they increased the roadblocks and their presence.

On March 4, 1973, AIM leaders said they would leave Wounded Knee if the U.S. government would also leave and allow the tribe to dissolve any conflicts themselves. The U.S. government officials demanded that the occupiers of Wounded Knee leave their weapons and identify themselves so they would not be subject to arrest. This had little effect.

On March 10, the U.S. government finally agreed to lift the roadblocks, which allowed AIM supporters to bring much-needed supplies into the town of Wounded Knee. Despite the lifting of the roadblocks, gunfire continued to be exchanged, and two people would die as a result: Frank Clearwater died of a wound he received while sleeping on a cot in an occupied church. Lawrence Lamont also died from a gunshot wound. It was Lamont's death that sparked a vital cease-fire.

Negotiations would continue for weeks, although a mutual agreement would never be reached. Nonetheless, by May 8, the majority of the AIM community had left Wounded Knee. The U.S.

government destroyed any security bunkers built by AIM members, along with the bunkers used by the marshals and the FBI. By the end of the day they had completed an entire evacuation of Wounded Knee.

Little evidence exists as to the exact numbers involved in the occupation. A few eyewitnesses claimed to have seen federal marshals, FBI agents, and armored vehicles. A journalist detailed sniper fire and federal helicopters and bullets flying in all directions.

Despite two fatalities and nearly three months of violence, many Sioux felt Wounded Knee was a victory against the U.S. government. They supported each other by offering food and assistance. They found pride in creating a network with fellow tribal members to get goods in and out of the occupied area.

In the aftermath, the U.S. government conducted hearings on the events and issues of Wounded Knee. They agreed to establish an Indian policy review committee. One of the main purposes was to look into the legal relationship between Native Americans and the U.S. government.

Despite the good intentions of the U.S. government, relations between Native Americans and authorities would continue to be dicey. Many arrests would be made, most without any sort of formal charges or convictions. Brutalities still occurred, and harassment was commonplace.

Today there are still many unanswered questions about what happened on the Pine Ridge Indian Reservation. Fortunately, there have been no further fatalities. But the tragedy still lingers on in the memories of the 28,000 people on the reservation.

GAMBLING IN DEADWOOD: THE WILD WEST IS STILL ALIVE

1989

The dusty dirt roads of Deadwood are long gone. The brothels have disappeared. It is safe to walk the streets again, with no fear of being shot down in a gunfight. Gone are the likes of Wild Bill Hickock, Calamity Jane, Jack McCall, Al Swearengen, and Seth Bullock. Because of its rich past, the entire town has been declared a National Historic Landmark.

Like the prospectors of its past, Deadwood's citizens took a risk on their future. In order to be closer to their Wild West roots, the citizens agreed to allow casino-style gambling. It wasn't long before throngs of visitors looking for a taste of the West's wild past came seeking fortune in the historic hamlet of Deadwood.

Tom Blair—a prominent figure in Deadwood's story of gambling, and cofounder of the You Bet Committee—put it this way:

> *From the beginning, the main goal was economic revitalization and historic restoration to the infrastructure*

*of Deadwood. It started in 1986, when I attended
a seminar in Hot Springs, and the emphasis of that
seminar was: "Don't reinvent yourself. Work with
what you already have." And what Deadwood had
plenty of was history. Obviously gambling was a
major contributor to Deadwood's history, and we
decided to let our history restore our future. So a
group of local businessmen and -women formed what
is now called Deadwood You Bet.*

In November of 1988 the voters of South Dakota passed a law that amended the constitution to allow a certain amount of small-stakes gambling. The kicker, however, was that South Dakotans could only allow gambling to occur in the town of Deadwood. A year later, the citizens of Deadwood were quite happy when South Dakotans, under the direction of the state legislature, voted for casino gambling in their town.

After a well-organized effort by the You Bet Committee, which included gathering over 36,000 signatures, the citizens of Deadwood had casinos, complete with tables and slot machines. Soon tourists from both in and out of state were headed to Deadwood for a taste of the Old West. Even though the first bets were capped at $5, the games were on.

Deadwood would become the gambling center of the Black Hills and South Dakota. Before the vote to allow gambling in Deadwood, the state allowed dog- and horse-race gambling. In 1987 South Dakota created a state-sponsored lottery. In 1989 the state also began electronic gaming at very specific age-restricted locations. Each video lottery location was allowed only twenty machines, and the odds were in favor of the player, *not* the machine. Soon the lottery allowed machines in more locations throughout the state. In 2000, voters of South Dakota attempted—but failed—to impose more restrictions.

Other casinos popped up in South Dakota, but they were limited to nine Native American casinos: Sisseton, Hankinson, Watertown, Wagner, Lower Brule, Mobridge, Fort Thompson, Pine Ridge, and Flandreau.

The Deadwood casinos were a huge hit with tourists and South Dakotans looking for a getaway—and perhaps looking to hit it big. At first each Deadwood casino was only permitted to have thirty games, whether they were machines or tables. This proved to be less than adequate, and the state legislature changed the law to allow for one location to have ninety games. The only games permitted were blackjack and poker.

Today, Deadwood has become the destination of choice for anyone who wants to experience a little of the Old West. In the evenings there are staged gunfights, and personalities from the past walk the streets, dressed in their regalia. But it is the thrill of perhaps taking home millions that keeps people coming to Deadwood.

As is the case in nearly every casino in the world, the house typically wins. For Deadwood and the state of South Dakota, this means increased revenue. Of the money made from the casinos, 8 percent of the winnings go to the state of South Dakota. Of that 8 percent, 40 percent of the money goes to tourist promotion to attract visitors to South Dakota, 10 percent to the city of Deadwood, and the remaining 50 percent to the state to regulate gambling. If the regulatory costs do not use all of that 50 percent, the remainder of the money goes to ensure the best historical presentation of Deadwood.

Outside of Deadwood, there are only a few other cities in the U.S. that allow full-scale casino gambling. On weekends the casinos are loaded with fortune seekers. One could even strike it rich while picking up some food for dinner, since the town's main grocery store has machines. During the summertime, the downtown area has the feel of Mardi Gras or Carnivale, as patrons spill out onto the streets adorned in everything from beads to cowboy hats to chaps. Gamblers will try anything to increase their luck.

The main "strip" is a brick-lined street with restored nineteenth-century buildings, including the three-story Bullock Hotel, built by Seth Bullock himself in 1895. Gamblers and visitors are also accustomed to gunfire—friendly fire, of course. Beginning on Memorial Day history is relived as actors in full dress pretend to be Wild Bill as he gets shot in the back. Jack McCall is constantly trying to outrun the vigilantes. McCall never gets caught; he usually winds up running into the arms of one of Deadwood's famous madams or sneaking off into one of the restored mining gulches.

Although the streets in Deadwood are safer now than they were when Jack McCall was truly "at large," there is still plenty of star power in Deadwood. Celebrities can often be seen here, and Kevin Costner, well-known actor, director, and producer, owns the Midnight Star Casino in downtown Deadwood. Adorning the walls of the Midnight Star are many items of movie memorabilia, along with props and costumes from all of Costner's movies.

Today, the entire town is designated as a National Historic Landmark. The gambling income, nearly $7 million a year, has preserved the history of the town, but it also provides better infrastructure for its citizens. Even if the gamblers in Deadwood walk away with less than they started with, the town of Deadwood and the state of South Dakota benefit.

DANCES WITH HOLLYWOOD: SOUTH DAKOTA HITS THE BIG SCREEN

1989

The air is thick with dust. Hot and dry, the South Dakota prairie sits baking in the July sun, with temperatures hovering near 100 degrees Fahrenheit. Flies buzz around the stench of fresh buffalo dung. As a light wind blows across the prairie grasses, the herd of buffalo begins to move. Faster and faster, they pick up their lope, until they are galloping at full speed. Soon, hunters surround their flanks . . . Kicking Bird, Wind in His Hair, Chief Ten Bears, and the lone non-Indian of the group, Lieutenant John J. Dunbar.

"Cut!" yells a voice through a distant megaphone. The buffalo settle back into a walk. The hunters now look more like stuntmen as they bring their horses to a trot and head back to the trailers, where they take off their traditional dress and head to the watercooler for a drink of ice water.

The setting is the Triple U Buffalo Ranch outside of Pierre, known to most folks in the area as the Houck Ranch. It is home to over 3,500 bison roaming on 60,000 acres. The ranch and its buffalo have been featured before, but it wasn't until Kevin Costner and his film crew came knocking that the buffalo herds roaming the ranch would become movie stars.

Dances with Wolves is an epic period movie detailing the trials of Lieutenant John J. Dunbar, a Civil War veteran turned U.S. Cavalry officer who requests a transfer to the western frontier. He is eventually alone at his post on the frontier and befriends members of a Sioux tribe. Dunbar is eventually adopted into the Sioux band, led by Chief Ten Bears (played by Floyd Red Crow Westerman). But in time the advancing troops from Fort Sedgewick are on the trail of Ten Bears' clan. Lieutenant Dunbar—who was given the name Dances with Wolves because members of Ten Bears' clan saw him cavorting with a wolf—now flees for fear his presence will cause further harm to Ten Bears' clan.

All but a few scenes of the movie were filmed in South Dakota, from July 18 to November 23, 1989. Locations used in the movie include Badlands National Park, the Black Hills, the Sage Creek Wilderness Area, and the Belle Fourche River area.

Costner wanted to use an accurate version of the Sioux language in the film. Despite simplifying the language to a certain extent, the language in the movie is close to an actual Lakota dialect. Costner had an on-site language instructor, Doris Leader Charge, who also played the role of Ten Bears' wife, Pretty Shield. She coached the other actors in this dialect (English subtitles were added for the viewers).

Similar to using a native dialect, in order to ensure accuracy, Costner chose to use live buffalo for the hunting scenes. The Triple U is the largest buffalo ranch in the country, so Costner had his pick of buffalo to use for the film. It is said, however, that the film crew borrowed two domesticated buffalo from recording artist Neil Young to use for the scenes where human-buffalo interactions were necessary.

The hunting scene in the movie was shot live on the Triple U. Costner insisted on doing his own stunts during the scene, and the only computer-generated effects or animation occurred when a buffalo was portrayed as being shot or wounded. Several cameras were loaded onto helicopters for a wide range of camera angles. And, although it may be surprising given the large number of animals used in the film, there were no injuries to any of the animals during the filming.

The Triple U Ranch was also home to many of the sets in the movie, including Dunbar's cabin, originally meant to be Fort Sedgewick. The early scenes in the movie with the wagon trains were also filmed on the ranch. The 60,000 acres of the ranch served as an ideal location. The vastness of the ranch allowed for camera angles and horizon shots to include entire landscapes, creating an accurate feel of the Western frontier.

Today, the vistas seen in the movie would look much the same as they did on the big screen. And, most likely, the look of the frontier at the time of the Sioux and the Cavalry would be similar to the current landscape of the Triple U Ranch; not much has changed since then. Costner felt that the wide-open landscape, rolling hills, and seemingly endless prairie of South Dakota would be an ideal setting for his film.

The setting for the film's final scene, however, is different from the rolling prairie of central South Dakota. In the movie, Dances with Wolves and his new wife, Stands with a Fist (played by Mary McDonnell), are leaving Ten Bears and his clan. Stands with a Fist, like Dances with Wolves, was also an adopted white member of the clan. As Dances with Wolves and Stands with a Fist are heading in one direction, Ten Bears is taking his clan to their winter camp, high in the mountains. By doing this, he is hoping to delay the eventual confrontation with the oncoming Cavalry.

These last scenes were shot in the Black Hills; the exact location is marked by a small road sign deep in the Black Hills National

Forest and is easily accessible. To find the site, travel Highway 14A (a designated National Scenic Byway) north of Roughlock Falls via Spearfish Canyon. Once in Spearfish Canyon, locate Forest Road 222, about 3 miles upstream of the Spearfish Canyon Resort.

As a film, *Dances with Wolves* gained volumes of respect in many ways. At the box office it earned over $400 million worldwide. It won several awards, including Academy Awards for Best Picture and Best Director (Kevin Costner). South Dakotans appreciated the fact that it also won the Oscar for Best Cinematography, because of the film's portrayal of their home state. The film also received a nomination for Best Art Direction.

Scholars and critics heralded the movie for its attempt to portray Native Americans in the most non-stereotypical way. They agree that it surpasses typical Hollywood films that depict Native Americans as "noble savages." Because of this sensitivity, Costner was adopted by the Sioux Nation as an honorary member. In 2007, the Library of Congress selected the film for preservation in the United States National Film Registry.

As with any good Hollywood story, rumors abound, and *Dances with Wolves* is no exception. The most prevalent rumor concerns talk of a sequel based on *The Holy Road*, written by *Dances with Wolves* author, Michael Blake, and published in 2001. *The Holy Road* begins a little over a decade after *Dances with Wolves* ended and recounts what happens when one of the three children of Stands with a Fist and Dances with Wolves is kidnapped by white rangers. Blake has written a film adaptation, and Hollywood is talking about whether Costner is involved in the project; the same rumors also attach Viggo Mortensen to a possible sequel.

If *The Holy Road* were to come to fruition, South Dakota would certainly dazzle movie audiences once again.

THE GREAT FLOOD

1993

For most of the previous fall, rain had fallen in parts of South Dakota where normally the fall meant bone-dry conditions. As farmers struggled to harvest their corn and sorghum in the rains and hunters slogged through muddy fields in search of birds and deer, the rain continued to fall. As fall moved into winter, snow fell. And fell. By New Year's Day, 1993, the soil, now covered in snow, was already saturated.

As the winter months of 1993 moved into the spring months of March and April, snow continued to fall, interspersed with heavy rains that blanketed the region when it wasn't snowing. Conditions were prime for wide-scale flooding. As if the winter snow and spring rains weren't enough, the month of May brought a rash of heavy storms to South Dakota, which proved to be enough to kick-start the massive flood that was about to occur.

On May 22, 1993, one major thunderstorm opened up over the eastern portion of the state, causing floods in five counties and creating widespread tornadoes that injured twelve people and proved fatal for one. The dark clouds camped over eastern South Dakota and rained, hailed, and wreaked havoc on the already-saturated ground. In a little over three hours, this storm dumped record amounts of rain—between 5 and 7.5 inches—in the Sioux Falls area . . . but that was not the end of it.

This large amount of rain fell at a time when the area was already waterlogged from the plentiful rains and snow of the previous fall and winter. And the rain didn't let up once summer rolled in. During the next three months, from May through July, eastern South Dakota would receive record amounts of moisture. Sioux Falls recorded 22.55 inches of rain during this ninety-day period, and over 33 inches overall for 1993. From July 1992 to July 1993, a total of 42.20 inches fell on Sioux Falls.

Following the tornado outbreak on May 22, another storm hit Sioux Falls later in the month, causing a flash flood. The flood resulted in widespread sewer backups throughout Sioux Falls and southeastern South Dakota. The water and sewers flooded over 180 basements and spilled onto city streets, creating rivers of water and muck that flowed down municipal roads and streets. All of the rain had to go somewhere, and into the Big Sioux River it went. The river, normally a clear-flowing, placid stream, had leapt its banks and was over a mile wide in most places.

Further west, the James River topped record levels due to the snowpack from North Dakota and the heavy rains there. Streets in Mitchell were flooded. "The years of 1993 and 1995 get mixed together, but I believe 1993 was the scariest one for Mitchell," said Tim McGannon, city public works director since 1990. "Water rushing from brim-full Dry Run Creek was channeled over Ohlman Street, and then flowed over the tops of Minnesota and Burr streets," McGannon said.

Tom Greenway, a member of the Davison County Commission in 1993, said the following about the small Dry Run Creek getting out of control. "It was the worst. We had 6 inches of rain in a 24-hour period." He described water flooding Main Street in Mount Vernon, washing out area roads and damaging numerous fence lines.

"There was a foot of water going through Wermers' Lounge on Main Street in downtown Mount Vernon," said county highway superintendent Rusty Weinberg, who at the time was a member of the road crew.

The Vermillion River also went out of its banks. Despite its relatively short length of 45 miles, the river flooded Yankton. People were seen "boating" down city streets, doing everything they could to save their possessions.

Members of the American Red Cross and the Army National Guard were dispatched to most affected areas in South Dakota during June and July. Sandbags were a common sight in every town east of the Missouri River. Citizens banded together to save homes and other property. Animal shelters were packed full of displaced pets.

With the waters of the Big Sioux, James, and Vermillion rivers raging, the muddy torrents had to flow somewhere, and people downstream were bracing for disaster. The water ran into the Missouri River, and eventually the Mississippi raged, flooding areas once thought to be safe from rising waters. Levees broke in Illinois, Missouri, and further downstream. The U.S. government closed the Mississippi River to commerce in early July, causing a loss of $2 million a day in revenue.

By late July the waters slowly began to recede in South Dakota; by August, much of the land was a sloppy mess of mud and debris. Thousands of acres of crops were damaged because of floodwaters. Towns were forced to spend millions on clean-up of buildings, streets, and parklands. South Dakota alone suffered four deaths; businesses suffered $2 million in damages to buildings and loss of revenue due to the floods; $12 million in damages to public facilities;

$10 million in damages to private homes and residences; and a staggering $204 million was lost by the agricultural industry. Roads and highways suffered as well, with eventual repairs topping $3 million.

Downstream of South Dakota, the damages were catastrophic. The Mississippi flooded for nearly 200 days in 1993; the Missouri, close to 100 days of flooding. It wasn't until October 7, 1993, that the Mississippi River dropped below flood stage.

The Great Flood of 1993 encompassed an area 745 miles long and about 435 miles wide, totaling 320,000 square miles. In this area the flooded region consisted of around 30,000 miles.

Portions of the Great Flood across the Midwest caused damage to approximately 10,000 homes, and fifteen million acres of farmland were flooded. Two towns in other states—Valmeyer, Illinois, and Rhineland, Missouri—had to be moved to higher ground.

Thirty-two people lost their lives as a result of the Great Flood, but many experts believe the death toll was even higher. The total cost in damages topped $15 billion. Hundreds of studies of the Great Flood have resulted in the construction of additional, higher-quality levees throughout the Missouri and Mississippi River corridors.

PLANE CRASH: LEARJET CRASH KILLS GOLFER PAYNE STEWART

1999

The farmlands near Aberdeen were quiet on October 25, 1999. Pheasants squawked in the fields. Cows mooed to each other. The occasional car drove past the tranquil setting alongside U.S. Highway 12 near Mina.

At the same time, nearly 3,500 miles to the south, well-known golfer Payne Stewart and five others boarded a Learjet 35 in Orlando, Florida, with a destination of Dallas, Texas. Stewart, a two-time U.S. Open champion known for his colorful pants, was headed to Texas to play in the PGA Championship. Along with Stewart, other passengers on board included the two pilots, Michael Kling and Stephanie Bellegarrigue, and Stewart's agents, Robert Fraley and Van Arden. Also on board was Bruce Borland, a well-known golf course architect working for the Jack Nicklaus golf design company.

As the plane took off, South Dakota Highway Patrol sergeant Scott Wherry was settling in for a normal day of patrolling the farm roads and small towns of north-central South Dakota.

Back over northern Florida, things took a turn for the worse. As the Learjet carrying Stewart and the other passengers cleared 39,000 feet, air traffic controllers with the Federal Aviation Administration (FAA) noted that the plane was experiencing "significant changes in altitude." They tried continuously to contact the cockpit of the Learjet, without success. The Pentagon was contacted, and the Learjet was soon being escorted by two Air Force F-16 fighters from Tyndall Air Force Base. The two F-16s could not reach the Learjet, but a third plane, an F-16 from Elgin Air Force Base, located the jet. The pilot noticed both engines were running and the exterior of the plane looked normal. He did not notice any flight control movement, however.

The fighter pilot couldn't see into the passenger section of the plane because the windows were too dark, but he could see the windows of the cockpit. He noted that the entire right cockpit windshield was opaque and gray in color. He also noticed that the left cockpit was similar in color, although a few sections were not as gray as others. Before he could surmise any more, the pilot diverted the F-16 to St. Louis for fear of running out of fuel.

Fifteen minutes passed and two F-16s from the Oklahoma Air National Guard near Tulsa were dispatched. The lead pilot reported similar conditions, although he couldn't tell if the windshield was iced or not. A few minutes passed before the pilot reported, "We're not seeing anything inside; could be just a dark cockpit, though . . . he is not reacting, moving or anything like that; he should [have been] able to [see] us by now." During this intercept the Learjet's altitude varied from 22,000 feet to 51,000 feet.

Finally, two F-16s from Fargo, North Dakota, made visual contact with the Learjet. The F-16s from Oklahoma also rejoined the intercept after refueling. Soon all four fighter pilots reported that the aircraft's windows were fogged with ice. They also reported a lack of any flight control capabilities. Less than twenty minutes later, the F-16s reported that the Learjet was entering into a spiral downfall.

At 12:13 local time, the Learjet crashed into the South Dakota farmland, hitting the ground at a near supersonic speed and a reported extreme angle. The flight time was three hours and fifty-four minutes.

Pressurization emergencies in a Learjet 35 are rare, as the jet is equipped with emergency oxygen to be used in the event that the pressurization system fails above 12,000 feet. The pilots are required to wear masks for this reason.

On the ground in Aberdeen, Wherry received a phone call alerting him to the F-16s and the Learjet's path. Wherry and his staff immediately went outside and looked up. There they were: the fighter planes and the ghostly Learjet.

"It appeared to [not] be flying in a straight line," Wherry said. "It was wavering. You could see by its trail it was not going in a straight line. Then it headed straight down, nose first."

A local witness, Terry Jundt, was on horseback when he came across the mass of metal and debris. When he saw the crash site, he said, "They are going to have a hard time finding anything or anybody in there."

It wasn't long before a team of investigators from the National Transportation Safety Board (NTSB) arrived at the scene. However, darkness had crept in, forcing them to postpone their investigation until the following morning.

Armed with heavy equipment the next day, NTSB investigators started to sift through the debris. The aircraft had left a crater about 30 to 40 feet in width and about 10 feet deep. Because of the sheer destruction of the crash and widespread scattering of debris, the investigation took several days.

According to the NTSB, "The probable cause of this accident was incapacitation of the flight crewmembers as a result of their failure to receive supplemental oxygen following a loss of cabin pressurization, for undetermined reasons." Their findings in the investigation continued:

> *Following the depressurization, the pilots did not receive supplemental oxygen in sufficient time and/or adequate concentration to avoid hypoxia and incapacitation. . . . [A] possible explanation for the failure of the pilots to receive emergency oxygen is that their ability to think and act decisively was impaired because of hypoxia before they could don their oxygen masks. No definitive evidence exists that indicates the rate at which the accident flight lost its cabin pressure; therefore, the Safety Board evaluated conditions of both rapid and gradual depressurization. . . . If there had been a breach in the fuselage (even a small one that could not be visually detected by the in-flight observers) or a seal failure, the cabin could have depressurized gradually, rapidly, or even explosively. . . . In summary, the Safety Board was unable to determine why the flight crew could not, or did not, receive supplemental oxygen in sufficient time and/or adequate concentration to avoid hypoxia and incapacitation.*

For months following the accident there were theories floating around that the Pentagon had given orders to "shoot down" the plane if it threatened a heavily populated area. But Air Force spokesman Captain Joe Della Vedova dismissed those rumors as quickly as they arose.

Memorials for Payne Stewart continued throughout the 1999 and 2000 golf seasons. At the 2000 U.S. Open, held at Pebble Beach, twenty-one of Stewart's fellow players simultaneously hit twenty-one balls into the ocean. In 2001 Stewart was posthumously inducted into the World Golf Hall of Fame.

ROARING GRIZZLY:
GRIZZLY GULCH FIRE BARELY
NIPS DEADWOOD

2002

Light snow fell on the gulches around Deadwood. Lucky gamblers counted their winnings, while those less fortunate scratched their heads and wondered when their luck might turn. Many in the town of Deadwood felt unlucky as well, but not because they had spent too much time at the tables; it was because several years of drought had not been broken.

Even as the snow fell, people knew it might be another summer of soot, flames, and heat as the Black Hills burned brown. As winter faded into spring and early summer became the heat of July, the lack of heavy winter snows and few hard spring rains resulted in the Black Hills becoming nearly desert-like in their aridity.

The citizens of Deadwood did have a reason to be positive, as the city had survived near destruction three times before. All three of these events—two massive fires and a major flash flood—had occurred within its first ten years as a town, so Deadwood remained optimistic despite the current drought. But had they ever seen a forest fire under these dry conditions?

During a ten-year span in the 1950s, the town saw over ten buildings destroyed by fire. They even lost a substantial portion of valuable historic records. In 1959 a fire blazed around Deadwood, destroying 4,500 acres and filling the city with smoke and ash. People evacuated and the city appeared doomed. Nonetheless, Deadwood escaped the flames and lived to thrive another day. In the 1980s, the city escaped fire again as several fires burned in the surrounding towns.

When news of a possible fire outbreak came to town in 2002, most citizens were cautiously optimistic. Mayor Francis Toscana noted that Deadwood had survived worse disasters.

On a high ridge south of Lead, on Monday, June 29, 2002, a large thunderstorm was brewing. As the sky darkened, flashes of lightning were seen by many onlookers. Unfortunately, as is the case with many summer thunderstorms, this one carried no rain, only lightning. As the strikes grew in intensity, one witness spotted rising plumes of smoke that soon turned into flames. The dangerously dry pine trees were quickly swallowed up in the blaze.

The exact cause of the fire is still in dispute. Many experts agree that lightning struck a power pole and caused an explosion. As firefighters responded to the area, they found a small fire underneath one of the power poles, which they quickly extinguished. But as they worked in the wind and heat of the ridge, the crew noticed a separate fire burning on the tops of the trees, growing ever fiercer with each gust of wind. As the flames and smoke engulfed the high ridge, the firefighters chose to evacuate the area for fear things could get worse and endanger the crew.

The fire continued to grow, and by Sunday it was moving in the direction of the towns of Lead and Deadwood. Evacuations of those towns began. More manpower was needed, so federal fire officials arrived to help the state's firefighters. Crews built a fire line on the north side of Lead, and firefighters worked into the night setting backfires, designed to burn up excess fuel. Airplanes and two helicopters were expected to arrive to assist the on-the-ground efforts. When they did they dropped water and retardant. State troopers were evacuating rural areas and monitoring roadblocks so that fire crews could more easily access fire lines and attack the fire.

All of this action occurred as the sky darkened, the winds grew in speed, and the fire inched its way toward Deadwood.

Although many of Deadwood's residents felt they would be safe thanks to the efforts of many local authorities and consistent news coverage, the town's frontier spirit fell by the wayside and thousands of residents, employees, and visitors chose to evacuate Deadwood and the surrounding areas. Nearly a thousand firefighters patrolled the city streets, insisting that residents evacuate. Most agreed and left without incident. Fortunately, their evacuation was short-lived, as the order was lifted by Monday afternoon when the fire was no longer raging out of control.

"Hours after we got word it was safe for us to return, a wave of vehicles descended upon town," said Deadwood's mayor, Francis Toscana. "The fire started on Saturday, the evacuation order was lifted Monday night, and by Tuesday it was business as usual." A few days later, Deadwood was covered with signs thanking law enforcement, firefighters, and everyone else who had assisted with fighting the fire.

From its start on June 29 to the point where it became controlled on July 7, the Grizzly Gulch Fire burned 11,589 acres of federal, state, and private land.

Since 2000, more than 137,000 acres of the Black Hills have burned. In 2002 alone, 168 fires burned a total of 13,892 acres. In

2001, 132 fires burned 30,568 acres. In 2000, one of the worst years on record, 204 fires burned 92,609 acres.

In 2002, from July 16 through 20, the Little Elk fire near Piedmont burned 673 acres of federal and private land. The Battle Creek fire burned from August 16 through 25, near Rockerville and Keystone, and burned 12,450 acres of federal and private land.

Forest fires continue to be a summer-long threat for much of the Black Hills. During years of mild winters, the dry conditions in the heavily forested Black Hills can create the perfect breeding ground for forest fires. Thankfully, through the efforts of many dedicated volunteers and forest managers, fires can now be better managed to protect people and their property.

SOUTH DAKOTA TIMELINE

900   Distant relatives of the Mandan, Hidatsa, and Arikara live in earth lodges, hunt the plains, and plant corn and sunflowers.

1500   Villages are dotted all along the Missouri River.

1700   Because of fur trappers, various goods arrive from Europe and are traded by the Mandan, Hidatsa, and Arikara. Horses and guns are brought into the area, greatly changing life on the plains.

1743   The La Verendrye brothers bury a lead tablet, claiming the land for France.

1760   The Sioux Indians first meet up with the Missouri River after being driven from Minnesota by the Chippewa. They clash with the Arikara, igniting a long war.

1794   The Sioux war with the Arikara ends after the Sioux successfully drive the Arikara from their original homelands.

1803   The Louisiana Purchase

1804–06   Lewis and Clark Expedition

1817   Joseph La Framboise builds his fur trading post near Fort Pierre.

1823   The Arikara and Ashley fight.

1825   Various treaties are signed with the Indian tribes in South Dakota.

1831   The *Yellowstone* becomes the first steamboat to travel on the Missouri River in South Dakota.

1838–39   Nicollet and Fremont conduct several exploratory expeditions through South Dakota.

1855–57   The U.S. Army buys Fort Pierre.

1855–57   Lieutenant G. K. Warren conducts explorations and surveys in Dakota and Nebraska, creating many of the first maps of the region.

1858   The Yankton Treaty is signed. The Sioux cede much of eastern South Dakota to the United States. White settlers continue to inhabit South Dakota.

1860–61   J.B.S. Todd, brother-in-law of Abraham Lincoln, heads to Washington to lobby for the creation of Dakota Territory.

1861   Dakota Territory is established.

1868   A treaty is signed with the Sioux, granting them much of the Black Hills as part of their reservation. This treaty was eventually broken by the U.S. government.

1874   Rumors of gold in the Black Hills start to filter out of the area.

1877   After an act of Congress on February 28, 1877, the U.S. government takes back more than 7 million acres of the Great Sioux Reservation.

1877   Crazy Horse is killed at Fort Robinson, Nebraska.

1888   A blizzard strikes South Dakota, killing over thirty-five people.

1890   Pierre is chosen as the state capital.

1890   The Massacre at Wounded Knee occurs.

1895   Walter William Taylor embezzles over $350,000 from the state treasury.

1904   Land on the Rosebud Indian Reservation is open for white settlement.

1906–07 The Chicago & Northwestern Railroad is built west from the Missouri River to Rapid City.

1927 Construction of Mount Rushmore begins.

1930s The Great Depression hits South Dakota extremely hard.

1939 Badlands National Monument is created.

1944 The Pick-Sloan Plan for the upper Missouri River is created.

1947 Construction begins on the Crazy Horse Memorial.

1952 A major flood proves the safety of the Pick-Sloan Act.

1962 The Oahe Dam is completed.

1962 The Pathfinder Atomic Plant is built, but only operates for one year as a nuclear plant.

1973 The FBI, the AIM, and U.S. Marshals descend onto the Pine Ridge Indian Reservation; months of standoffs ensue.

1980 The Chicago, Milwaukee, St. Paul, and Pacific railroads all abandon thousands of miles of track.

1987 The South Dakota Lottery is created.

1987 A fire consumes an entire block of Deadwood.

1988 Citizens vote to approve limited casino gambling in Deadwood.

1993 One of the worst floods in U.S. history hits South Dakota.

1993 Governor Mickelson dies in a plane crash in Iowa.

1999 Plane crash near Aberdeen kills Payne Stewart and others and ignites a major investigation.

2000 Sturgis Motorcycle Rally attendance tops 750,000.

2002 Fire nearly destroys Deadwood—again.

2007 Site near Lead is open as possible new gold mine.

MOUNT RUSHMORE TIMELINE

1885   Charles Rushmore visits the Black Hills to inspect mining claims, and Mount Rushmore is given his name.

1923   Doane Robinson writes to Lorado Taft, asking for his thoughts on carving The Needles into the likeness of a "notable Sioux such as Red Cloud" and other Western figures.

1924   Robinson contacts Gutzon Borglum, who is enthusiastic. To ensure national interest, Borglum insists on including George Washington and Abraham Lincoln as subjects.

1925   South Dakota signs the Mount Harney National Memorial bill, allowing the carving in Custer State Park.
Aug.: Borglum visits South Dakota and determines that Mount Rushmore is more suitable than The Needles. He also adds Thomas Jefferson and Theodore Roosevelt to the plans for his monument.
Oct. 1: Mount Rushmore is dedicated.

1927   President Calvin Coolidge spends the summer in the Black Hills, and a second dedication occurs with Coolidge present.
Oct. 4: Actual carving begins.

1930   July 4: Washington's head is dedicated.

1931   Workers carving Jefferson's head encounter problems when they discover a massive crack; they are concerned about future work in that area.

1933   Gutzon's son Lincoln Borglum begins full-time work at Rushmore.

Several tons of stone are removed to create room for Jefferson's face. The new location is on the opposite side of Washington. The old face is blasted away.

1935   A surface for Roosevelt's face is found. Jefferson's lip is patched.

1936   The monument is under the jurisdiction of the National Park Service. Julian Spotts is hired to work with Borglum.

Aug. 30: President Roosevelt attends the dedication of Jefferson's head.

1937   A bill is introduced in the U.S. Congress to carve a head of Susan B. Anthony. Later in the session, a Congress rider requires that money be spent only on those figures already begun.

Sept. 17: Lincoln is dedicated.

1938   Work focuses on Roosevelt, with work beginning on Washington's neck.

1939   July 2: Roosevelt's head is dedicated. Special lighting effects are used to stage the dedication of the Roosevelt head.

1941   March 6: Borglum dies in Chicago due to complications from surgery.

Lincoln Borglum is on-site to finish the remaining work on the heads.

Oct. 31: Last day of carving.

SOUTH DAKOTA FACTS AND TRIVIA

State Capital: Pierre
Largest City: Sioux Falls
Size: 77,121 square miles (seventeenth-largest state, geographically)
Population: 775,933 (2005 Census Bureau); National rank, 46
Name for Residents: South Dakotans
Highest Point: Harney Peak, 7,242 feet above sea level
Lowest Point: Big Stone Lake, 962 feet above sea level
Origin of the State Name: "Dakota" is how the Sioux Indians referred to themselves
Indian Tribes: Home to nine official tribes
State Nickname: The Mount Rushmore State
State Motto: "Under God the people rule"
State Song: "Hail, South Dakota"
Dinosaur Fossils Found: Anatotitan, Camptosaurus, Denversaurus, Edmontosaurus, Hoplitosaurus, Iguanodon, Nanotyrannus, Pachycephalosaurus, Thescelosaurus, Thespesius, Torosaurus, Triceratops (state fossil), Tyrannosaurus
State Fossil: Triceratops
State Flag: Adopted in 1963
State Mammal: Coyote
State Fish: Walleye
State Insect: Honeybee
State Flower: American pasqueflower (the May Day flower)
State Tree: Black Hills Spruce

State Mineral: Rose quartz

State Gemstone: Fairburn agate, originally found near Fairburn

State Jewelry: Black Hills gold

State Soil: Houdek

BIBLIOGRAPHY

Mystery in the Mud: The Crow Creek Massacre—1350

Hogan, Edward Patrick. *South Dakota: An Illustrated Geography.* Huron, SD: East Eagle Co., 1991.

Kivett, Marvin F., and R. E. Jensen. "Archaeological Investigations at the Crow Creek Site" (39BF11), *Nebraska State Historical Society Publications in Anthropology,* 7, 1976.

Willey, P. *Prehistoric Warfare on the Great Plains: Skeletal Analysis of the Crow Creek Massacre Victims.* New York: Garland, 1990.

Willey, P., and Thomas E. Emerson. "The Osteology and Archaeology of the Crow Creek Massacre," *Plains Anthropologist,* 38 (145): 227–269, 1993.

Zimmerman, Larry J. *Peoples of Prehistoric South Dakota.* Lincoln and London: University of Nebraska Press, 1985.

———. "Understanding Conflict and Warfare," Lecture 6 Notes, Crow Creek Case Study, www.larryjzimmerman.com/warfare/lec6.html, accessed January 20, 2009.

The La Verendrye Brothers: Their Short-Lived French Claim—1743

Kingsbury, George Washington. *History of Dakota Territory.* Chicago: The S. J. Clarke Publishing Company, 1915. Original reprint from the New York Public Library.

Malone, Michael, and Richard Roeder. *Montana: A History of Two Centuries.* Seattle: University of Washington Press, 1991.

Tubbs, Stephenie Ambrose, with Clay Straus Jenkinson. *The Lewis and Clark Companion: An Encyclopedic Guide to the Voyage of Discovery.* New York: Henry Holt & Company, 2003.

Wallace, W. Stewart, ed. *The Encyclopedia of Canada,* Vol. IV. Toronto: University Associates of Canada, 1948.

First Vote West of the Mississippi—1804

Ambrose, Stephen. *Undaunted Courage: Meriwether Lewis, Thomas Jefferson, and the Opening of the American West.* New York: Simon & Schuster, 1997.

Burns, Ken, and Dayton Duncan. *Lewis & Clark: The Journey of the Corps of Discovery.* New York: Knopf, 1997.

Tubbs, Stephenie Ambrose, with Clay Straus Jenkinson. *The Lewis and Clark Companion: An Encyclopedic Guide to the Voyage of Discovery.* New York: Henry Holt & Company, 2003.

La Framboise and Fort Pierre: First Permanent Settlement in South Dakota—1817

Hudson, John C. *Across This Land: A Regional Geography of the United States and Canada.* Baltimore, MD: The Johns Hopkins University Press, 2002.

Ostler, Jeffrey. *The Plains Sioux and U.S. Colonialism from Lewis and Clark to Wounded Knee.* New York: Cambridge University Press, 2004.

Schell, Herbert S. *History of South Dakota.* Pierre: South Dakota State Historical Society, 2004.

Silvestro, Roger. *In the Shadow of Wounded Knee: The Untold Story of the Indian Wars.* New York: Roger L. Walker and Company, 2005.

Arikara and Ashley: The First Fight—1823

Clarke, Charles G., and Dayton Duncan. *The Men of the Lewis & Clark Expedition.* Lincoln: University of Nebraska Press / Bison Books, 2002.

Hafen, LeRoy, Harvey Carter, and A. H. Clark. *Trappers of the Far West: Sixteen Biographical Sketches.* Lincoln: University of Nebraska Press, 1983.

Schell, Herbert S. *History of South Dakota.* Pierre: South Dakota State Historical Society, 2004.

Utley, Robert. *After Lewis and Clark: Mountain Men and the Paths to the Pacific.* Lincoln: University of Nebraska Press, 2004.

Wishart, David. *Encyclopedia of the Great Plains: A Project of the Center for Great Plains Studies.* Lincoln: University of Nebraska Press, 2004.

Todd the Lobbyist: Dakota Territory Is Established—1861

Barbour, Barton H. *Fort Union and the Upper Missouri Fur Trade.* Norman: University of Oklahoma Press, 2001.

Lamar, Howard. *Dakota Territory, 1861–1889: A Study of Frontier Politics.* New Haven, CT: Yale University Press, 1956.

———, ed. *The New Encyclopedia of the American West,* p. 282. New Haven, CT: Yale University Press, 1998.

Smith, George Martin, ed. *History of Dakota Territory—South Dakota: Its History and Its People,* Vol. II. Chicago: The S. J. Clarke Publishing Company, 1915.

Custer's Gold! Gold Discovered in the Black Hills—1874

McDermott, John. *Gold Rush: The Black Hills Story.* Pierre: South Dakota State Historical Society, 2001.

Monaghan, Jay. *Custer: The Life of General George Armstrong Custer.* Lincoln: University of Nebraska Press, 1971.

Parker, Watson. *Gold in the Black Hills.* Lincoln: University of Nebraska Press, 1966.

Wolf, David. www.blackhillsvisitor.com, accessed January 25, 2009.

Deadwood: South Dakota's Tall-Tale Factory—1876

Ames, John Edward. *The Real Deadwood: True Life Histories of Wild Bill Hickok, Calamity Jane, Outlaw Towns, and Other Characters of the Lawless West.* New York: Chamberlain Brothers, 2004.

Hudson, John C. *Across This Land: A Regional Geography of the United States and Canada.* Baltimore, MD: The Johns Hopkins University Press, 2002.

Lee, Bob. *Gold, Gals, Guns, Guts: A History of Deadwood, Lead, and Spearfish, 1874–1976.* Pierre: South Dakota State Historical Society Press, 2004.

McClintock, John. *Pioneer Days in the Black Hills: Accurate History and Facts Related by One of the Early Day Pioneers.* Norman: University of Oklahoma Press, 2000.

Parker, Watson. *Deadwood: The Golden Years.* Lincoln: University of Nebraska Press / Bison Books, 1981.

Rosa, Joseph. *Wild Bill Hickok: The Man and His Myth.* Lawrence: University Press of Kansas, 1996.

Blown Away: The First Tornado Ever Photographed—1884

Baum, L. Frank. *Our Landlady.* Edited and annotated by Nancy Tystad Koupal. Lincoln: University of Nebraska Press, 1996.

Goertz, Reuben. "The Legacy of the First American Tornado Ever Photographed, Dakota Territory, 1884" (unpublished paper). Sioux Falls, SD: Center for Western Studies, Augustana College.

Janzen, Rod. *The Prairie People: Forgotten Anabaptists.* Lebanon, NH: University Press of New England, 1999.

Mogil, Michael. *Extreme Weather: Understanding the Science of Hurricanes, Tornadoes, Floods, Heat Waves, Snow Storms, Global*

Warming and Other Atmospheric Disturbances. New York: Black Dog and Leventhal Publishers, 2007.

Svenvold, Mark. *Big Weather: Chasing Tornadoes in the Heart of America.* New York: Henry Holt & Company, 2005.

January Blizzard: South Dakota's Fatal Snow Day—1888

"The Blizzard of 1888," Nebraska State Historical Society, www.nebraskahistory.org/publish/markers/texts/blizzard_of_1888.htm, accessed February 10, 2009.

Laskin, David. *The Children's Blizzard.* New York: HarperCollins, 2005.

Robinson, Doane. *A Brief History of South Dakota.* Charleston, SC: BiblioBazaar, 2008.

"This Day in History 1888: Blizzard Tragedy to Northwest Plains," History.com, www.history.com/this-day-in-history.do?action=Article&id=52886, accessed February 10, 2009.

The Last Indian: The Death of Sitting Bull—1890

Allison, Edwin Henry. *The Surrender of Sitting Bull.* Charleston, SC: BiblioLife, 2008.

Anderson, Gary. *Sitting Bull and the Paradox of Lakota Nationhood,* 2nd ed. White Plains, NY: Longman, 2006.

Brown, Dee. *Bury My Heart at Wounded Knee: An Indian History of the American West.* New York: Henry Holt & Company, 2001.

Roop, Peter, and Connie Roop. *Sitting Bull.* New York: Scholastic Paperbacks, 2002.

Viola, Herman. *Trail to Wounded Knee: The Last Stand of the Plains Indians, 1860–1890.* Washington, DC: National Geographic Society, 2003.

Yenne, Bill. *Sitting Bull.* Yardley, PA: Westholme Publishing, 2009.

Tragedy at Wounded Knee: Massacre and Conquest of the Sioux—1890

Anderson, Gary. *Sitting Bull and the Paradox of Lakota Nationhood,* 2nd ed. White Plains, NY: Longman, 2006.

Brown, Dee. *Bury My Heart at Wounded Knee: An Indian History of the American West.* New York: Henry Holt & Company, 2001.

Coleman, William. *Voices of Wounded Knee.* Lincoln: University of Nebraska Press / Bison Books, 2001.

Jensen, Richard, Eli Paul, and John Carter. *Eyewitness at Wounded Knee.* Lincoln: University of Nebraska Press, 1991.

Mooney, James. *The Ghost-Dance Religion and Wounded Knee.* Mineola, NY: Dover Publications, 1991.

Robinson, Doane. *A Brief History of South Dakota.* Charleston, SC: BiblioBazaar, 2008.

Silvestro, Roger. *In the Shadow of Wounded Knee: The Untold Story of the Indian Wars.* New York: Roger L. Walker and Company, 2005.

Viola, Herman. *Trail to Wounded Knee: The Last Stand of the Plains Indians, 1860–1890.* Washington, DC: National Geographic Society, 2003.

Capital Complex: Mitchell and Pierre Fight over Seat of Government—1904

"A Capital Fight: Choosing South Dakota's Capital City," South Dakota State Historical Society traveling exhibit, www.sdhistory .org/mus/mus_trav.htm.

"The Great Capitol Fight of 1904," South Dakota State Historical Society, www.sdhistory.org/Exhibit4/arc_lov_capfight.htm, accessed February 20, 2009.

Our Statehouse: A Capitol Idea, television broadcast, South Dakota Public Broadcasting, 2008.

Too Corny: The World's Only Corn Palace—1921

Cerney, Jan. *Images of America: Mitchell's Corn Palace.* Charleston, SC: Arcadia Publishing, 2004.

Mitchell Chamber of Commerce. *A Year by Year History of . . . The World's Only Corn Palace,* 5th ed. Mitchell, SD: Educator Supply Company, 1957.

Rubin, Cynthia Elyce. "The Midwestern Corn Palaces: A 'Maize' of Detail and Wonder," *The Clarion* (Fall 1983): 24–31.

The Greatest Monument Never Finished: Mount Rushmore—1927

Modern Marvels: Mount Rushmore (DVD). The History Channel, 2005.

Smith, Rex Alan. *The Carving of Mount Rushmore.* New York: Abbeville Press, 1994.

Taliaferro, John. *Great White Fathers: The True Story of Gutzon Borglum and His Obsessive Quest to Create the Mt. Rushmore National Monument.* New York: PublicAffairs, 2004.

Pardon, Madam: Poker Alice Saved from Prison—1928

Enss, Chris. *The Lady Was a Gambler.* Guilford, CT: Globe Pequot Press, 2007.

Fielder, Mildred. *Poker Alice.* Deadwood, SD: Centennial Distributors, 1978.

Rutter, Michael. *Upstairs Girls.* Helena, MT: Farcountry Press, 2005.

Burning Up the Track: "Smokey" Joe Mendel Wins State Track Meet—1931

"Smokey" Joe Mendel, Hall of Fame Profile. South Dakota Sports Hall of Fame, www.sdshof.com, accessed February 20, 2009.

Waltner, Tim. *The Times and Life of Smokey Joe Mendel.* Freeman, SD: Pine Hill Press, 1992.

Thirsty? Wall Drug Serves Settlers—1931

"Wall and Water," *Guideposts.* Carmel, NY: Guideposts Associates, Inc., 1982.

The Wall Drug Story. Wall Drug, 2008.

Rally 'Em Up: The Sturgis Motorcycle Rally Begins—1938

Higgins, Michelle. "The Real Easy Rider," *New York Times,* August 5, 2005.

"History of Sturgis Rally," Jackpine Gypsies, www.jackpine-gypsies .com/history.html, accessed February 20, 2009.

"Pappy Hoel," AMA Motorcycle Hall of Fame Museum, www .motorcyclemuseum.org/halloffame/hofbiopage.asp?id=198, accessed January 13, 2009.

Sturgis Rally Daily, www.sturgisrallydaily.com/.

Truly Great Badlands: President Roosevelt Creates Badlands National Monument—1939

de Girardin, E. "A Trip to the Bad Lands in 1849," *South Dakota Historical Review,* 1936.

Jackson-Washabaugh County Historical Society. "Interview of A. E. Johnson of Interior, SD, by John W. Stockert, January 30, 1968," *Jackson-Washabaugh Counties 1915–1965.*

Schell, Herbert S. *History of South Dakota.* Pierre: South Dakota
State Historical Society, 2004.

A Mountain of a Monument: Crazy Horse Memorial—1948

"Crazy Horse Memorial Fund Drive to Begin," Associated Press,
August 21, 2006.

DeWall, Rob. *Carving a Dream,* 8th rev. ed. Crazy Horse, SD:
Korczak's Heritage, 2007.

Higbee, Paul. "Carving Crazy Horse," *American Profile,* April 27,
2001.

Power Play: Oahe Dam Is Completed—1962

Lamar, Howard R., ed. *The New Encyclopedia of the American West,*
p. 282. New Haven, CT: Yale University Press, 1998.

Lawson, Michael L. *Dammed Indians: The Pick-Sloan Plan and
the Missouri River Sioux, 1944–1980.* Norman: University of
Oklahoma Press, 1982.

Lazarus, Edward. *Black Hills, White Justice: The Sioux Nation versus
the United States, 1775 to the Present.* New York: HarperCollins,
1991.

Shaky Year: The Earthquakes of 1964

Ansfield, Val. "Pamphlet on South Dakota Earthquakes." South
Dakota Geological Survey.

Chadima, Sarah. "South Dakota Earthquakes." Vermillion:
University of South Dakota, 1992. South Dakota State
Historical Society, 2004.

Hasselstrom, Linda. *Roadside History of South Dakota.* Missoula,
MT: Mountain Press Publishing, 1994.

"Minor Earthquake Detected in South Dakota," *Insurance Journal,* February 12, 2007. Insurance Journal, www.insurancejournal .com/news/midwest/2007/02/12/76864.htm, accessed February 25, 2009.

Black Hills Run Brown: The Rapid City Flood—1972

"At Least 105 Dead, $100 Million Damage," *Rapid City Journal,* June 11, 1972.

Barnett, Don (Rapid City mayor). Address to students at Waubay Junior High School, Waubay, SD, June 4, 2007.

"The Flood of 1972—20 Years Later," *Rapid City Journal,* May 17, 1992.

"Hills Storm Was a 100-year Rarity," *Rapid City Journal,* June 11, 1972.

"The 1972 Black Hills–Rapid City Flood Revisited," United States Geological Survey, http://sd.water.usgs.gov/projects/1972flood/, accessed October 22, 2008.

Reinjured: Wounded Knee II—1973

"Inside Wounded Knee," *Minneapolis Star Tribune,* March 25, 1973.

Reinhardt, Akim D. *Ruling Pine Ridge: Oglala Lakota Politics from the IRA to Wounded Knee.* Lubbock, TX: Texas Tech University Press, 2007.

Sayer, John William. *Ghost Dancing the Law: The Wounded Knee Trials.* Cambridge, MA: Harvard University Press, 1995.

A Tattoo on My Heart: The Warriors of Wounded Knee 1973. Badlands Films, 2004.

Williams, Lee. "FBI Explains 57 Unsolved Indian Deaths," *Argus Leader,* July 11, 2000.

Gambling in Deadwood: The Wild West Is Still Alive—1989

Robinson, Doane. *A Brief History of South Dakota*. Charleston, SC: BiblioBazaar, 2008.

Thompson, William Norman. *Gambling in America: An Encyclopedia of History, Issues and Society*. Santa Barbara, CA: ABC-CLIO, 2001.

Werner, Shawn. "A Fight for Gaming," *Deadwood Magazine*, www .deadwoodmagazine.com/back_issues/article.php?read_id=181, accessed March 2009.

Dances with Hollywood: South Dakota Hits the Big Screen—1989

Blake, Michael. *Dances with Wolves*. New York: Ballantine Books, 2001.

The Official Website of Michael Blake, http://danceswithwolves .net/home.php.

Svetkey, Benjamin. "Little Big Movie," *Entertainment Weekly*, March 8, 1991.

The Great Flood—1993

Chagnon, Stanley. *The Great Flood of 1993: Causes, Impacts, and Responses*. Boulder, CO: Westview Press, 1996.

Jehl, Douglas. "Clinton Hails Midwest Courage against the Flood," *New York Times*, August 13, 1993.

"Milestones," *Time Magazine*, December 20, 2004.

Uchitelle, Michelle. "The Midwest Flooding: Effects on Business; U.S. Economy Too Vast to Be Hurt by Flooding," *New York Times*, July 14, 1993.

Plane Crash: Learjet Crash Kills Golfer Payne Stewart—1999

"Golfer Payne Stewart Dies in Plane Crash," *Washington Post,* October 26, 1999.

"Minor Injuries Reported in South Dakota Plane Crash," *Sioux City Journal,* August 4, 2008.

"New Evidence: Payne Stewart's Plane Lost Pressure before Crash," CNN.com, posted November 23, 1999, http://edition.cnn.com/US/9911/23/stewart.crash.03/, accessed February 15, 2009.

"Payne Stewart Dead at 42," *CNN Sports Illustrated,* posted October 26, 1999, http://sportsillustrated.cnn.com/golf/pga/news/1999/10/25/stewart_plane_ap/index.html, accessed February 15, 2009.

Roaring Grizzly: Grizzly Gulch Fire Barely Nips Deadwood—2002

"City of Sin and Ashes," *Deadwood Magazine,* 2002, www.deadwoodmagazine.com/archivedsite/Archives/Ashes.htm.

"Memories Still Fresh for Victims of Grizzly Gulch Fire," *Rapid City Journal,* June 23, 2003.

"Volunteers Keep the Ball Rolling," *Rapid City Journal,* June 29, 2003.

INDEX

INDEX

Thunderhead Mountain sculptures, 91–95

Todd, John Blair Smith, 21–23, 135

tornadoes, 34–38

Toscana, Francis, 131, 132

track stars, 74–76

trading posts, 13–16

Trail of Broken Treaties, 109

treaties, 22, 24–25, 28, 45, 108, 135

Triple U Buffalo Ranch, 117–20

Tubbs, Warren G., 70

Utter, Charlie, 31

Utter, Steve, 31

Wall Drug, 77–80

Warren, G. K., 135

Weinberg, Rusty, 123

Wherry, Scott, 125, 127

Willard, Alexander, 10

Williams, J. J., 31

Wilson, Mrs., 42

Wilson, Richard A., 109–10

Wonderful Wizard of Oz, The (Baum), 34–36, 38

Wounded Knee II, 108–12

Wounded Knee Massacre, 50–54, 135

Wovoka, 45

Wright, Frank Lloyd, 89–90

Yankton, South Dakota, 21–22, 59, 97

Yankton Treaty, 22, 134

Ziolkowski, Korczak, 91–95

ABOUT THE AUTHOR

Patrick Straub has traveled extensively in South Dakota for nearly five years and has gained an appreciation for the state's unique history. He is the author of three books: *Montana: An Explorer's Guide*, *Montana on the Fly: An Angler's Guide*, and *The Orvis Pocket Guide to Streamer Fishing* (Globe Pequot Press). He lives with his wife, their two spoiled dogs, and four barn cats on the Bighorn River in southeastern Montana.